C000082440

Hidden Herefordshire

A Book of Country Walks
by
Julie Meech

Meridian Books

Published 1992 by Meridian Books

© Julie Meech 1992

ISBN 1-869922-16-6

A catalogue record for this book is available from the British Library.

The right of Julie Meech to be identified as the author of this work has been asserted by her in accordance with the Copyright, Designs and Patents Act 1988.

All rights reserved. No part of this publication may be copied, reproduced or transmitted in any form or by any means without the prior written permission of the publishers.

Publishers' Note

Every care has been taken in the preparation of this book. As far as possible the walks have been independently checked and are believed to be correct at the time of publication. However, neither the author nor the publishers can accept responsibility for any errors or omissions or for any loss, damage, injury or inconvenience resulting from the use of the book.
Please remember that the countryside is continually changing: hedges and fences may be removed or re-sited; landmarks may disappear; footpaths may be re-routed or be ploughed over and not reinstated (as the law requires); concessionary paths may be closed. The publishers would be very pleased to have details from users of this book of any changes that are observed or of difficulties that are encountered.

Meridian Books
40 Hadzor Road
Oldbury
Warley
West Midlands
B68 9LA

Printed in Great Britain by BPCC Wheatons Ltd., Exeter.

Contents

About the Author

Julie Meech was born in 1958 and grew up in Cheshire and Northumberland. For the last seven years she has lived in a small country cottage a few miles west of Worcester which she shares with two cats. A history graduate from the University of Exeter and an Associate of the Royal Photographic Society, she is now a freelance photographer and writer, supplying mainly magazines and books and specialising in wildlife, landscape and adventure travel. She writes a weekly column, *Walkabout*, for the *Worcester Evening News*.

Her interests include wildlife; conservation; environment; Third World; countryside; photography; vernacular architecture; local history; house/cottage restoration; books; old maps; travel, especially independent adventure travel; Africa and all things African.

Julie is a vegetarian and, although living in the country and travelling widely, manages to survive without a car.

Introduction

Pick up almost any guide to Herefordshire and you will notice the same phrases recurring — 'gentle, rolling countryside', 'a patchwork of green fields and softly rounded hills', 'quintessential England', and so on. Of course, all these things are true of Herefordshire, but there is a great deal more to it than this, and perhaps these writers should be made to struggle along the Black Mountain ridge on a winter's day when the cloud is down and the snow swirling madly in the vicious wind!

Pretty black and white villages slumbering under blue skies, set in blossom-laden apple orchards and surrounded by contented cows munching away in lush water meadows may be how many of us picture both Herefordshire and England, but such scenes are far from representative of either. Herefordshire, in fact, as every Welshman already knows, really belongs to two countries, and on the more rugged western edge you will find that the Welsh influence is as strong as the English, whether it be in respect of the landscape, the climate or the people.

Herefordshire consists of a central plain broken by a substantial river system and numerous low hills, the whole surrounded by a ring of more impressive hills, each with their own characteristics. This makes for a varied landscape, about which it is difficult to generalise. Further variety is added by the many different land uses. Although the arable prairie has well and truly arrived there are few places where it dominates the landscape and mixed farming survives throughout. Although orchards and hopyards are not so extensive as they used to be many do still remain to add further interest. There are few large woodlands, but there is a multitude of small woods and coppices which, together with some ancient hedgerows, effectively break up the landscape. Forestry is important too, and conifer plantations add another, not always welcome, element to the scene.

This book aims to reflect something of this variety. The walks are spread throughout the county and have been chosen to show as many different aspects of it as possible. You will notice one or two omissions such as the Malvern Hills and the Wye Valley — except for a brief foray to Bredwardine in a walk over Merbach Hill. This is because these areas are already well-known; the Malverns, to which Worcestershire has the largest claim anyway, are visited by hundreds of walkers every week, while the Wye Valley is Herefordshire's tourist Mecca and already more than adequately covered by the many books available.

NB: When local government reorganisation took place in 1974 Herefordshire was joined to Worcestershire in what has always been an uneasy marriage. Few people were impressed by this and in practical terms it has made little difference. This book deals only with the old county of Herefordshire, and there is some prospect that, at the forthcoming re-reorganisation in 1994, Herefordshire will again exist as a separate entity in name as well as in fact.

Julie Meech

To my mum, Jean, with love

What to take with you

For most of Herefordshire, most of the year, no special clothing or kit is required. Many of these walks could be done in trainers, and a light cagoule will usually be sufficient protection against the weather. On the other hand, many paths do become churned up by horses or cattle and you may find yourself wading through liquid mud, especially in winter. Proper walking boots will keep your feet dry in such conditions and offer good ankle support at all times, important on rough paths or difficult descents. The latest lightweight boots are very comfortable.

Walks in the Black Mountains should not be undertaken lightly. It may be warm and sunny when you set out but there is no guarantee that it will stay that way, and the winds can be unexpectedly ferocious, even when the valleys are calm. Always carry a small rucksack with extra clothing. In normal conditions there is little chance of getting lost in Herefordshire's Black Mountains; the way ahead, or escape routes down, are always obvious. If the mist should descend, however, it is another matter, and a compass could be invaluable.

This book should prevent you from getting lost, but a map could add greatly to your enjoyment, enabling you to put the whole scene in context and to identify distant views. It also means that you can shorten or lengthen or change any route as you desire. Ordnance Survey Landranger maps are suitable for many purposes but the Pathfinder series is immeasurably superior. The wealth of detail is an aid not only to navigation but also to actually understanding your surroundings.

A pair of binoculars can also help you to get more out of a walk. The new lightweight models fit easily into a pocket and even the cheapest offer more than adequate quality for the casual user.

A pair of secateurs will be useful if you encounter overgrowth – and if, as you walk along, you can snip off brambles and branches that are starting to intrude you will help to maintain the paths in a walkable state.

Abbreviations used in the text

FC   Forestry Commission

HNT   Herefordshire Nature Trust. The local organisation which seeks to protect the county's wildlife. The Trust owns and manages nature reserves, advises local councils on planning matters, and attempts to stimulate interest in and awareness of local wildlife and habitats. A member of the Royal Society for Nature Conservation (RSNC) Wildlife Trusts Partnership. Membership of HNT gives access to reserves not open to the public. For details contact HNT at 25 Castle Street, Hereford HR1 2NW.

HWCC   Hereford and Worcester County Council.

NCC   Nature Conservancy Council. Until 1991 this was the government agency with responsibility for conservation throughout Great Britain. It has now been split into three separate bodies: in England this means that we must now call it English Nature. It is, however, still better known by its former title and this may still be seen on notice boards.

NNR   National Nature Reserve. An example of a prime natural history habitat. Managed and wardened by English Nature, formerly NCC.

NT   National Trust.

RSPB   Royal Society for the Protection of Birds.

SSSI   Site of Special Scientific Interest. An area, large or small, which is of importance for its natural history or geology. Designated by English Nature. Many sites are privately owned and are being lost or damaged at a great rate — one of the worst culprits is the Department of Transport with its road-building frenzy.

TIC   Tourist Information Centre.

Public Transport

This book may appear to have been designed for the motorist, with circular routes and suitable parking places specified. This, however, is merely to recognise the realities of travel today, and, in fact, the book was designed more with the non-motorist in mind; the starting point was, in almost every case, dictated by the available bus services and the only place which is actually rather difficult to reach by bus is Much Marcle.

On a global scale, the pollution caused by the ever-increasing number of cars is one of the biggest problems facing the world today. At a more local level, it is becoming difficult to find anywhere in the English countryside which is entirely free of traffic noise, and many a potentially splendid view is blighted by the presence of parked cars. This is true as much of rural Herefordshire as of anywhere else. Weobley, in particular, springs to mind; take a look at Weobley's main street and then walk along the footpath to Dilwyn and you will understand exactly what I mean.

So, how about leaving the car at home once in a while? Country buses can be great fun; you'll meet some marvellous characters and you'll see the countryside at a more leisurely pace. You won't have to worry about parking, theft, or losing the keys. You can enjoy a drink in the pub, and you don't always have to restrict yourself to circular walks.

I only wish I could suggest you take the train as this would be even more environmentally friendly. Sadly, train services now have little relevance so far as access to Herefordshire's countryside is concerned. Once there were forty-three stations, now there are four. If we do not use our country buses they will go the same way. Many already have, others exist only because they are subsidised by HWCC. On the other hand, if we create a demand the operators will be only too pleased to provide a service.

Because Herefordshire is served by a multitude of local operators the best way to obtain information about services is to consult the excellent timetable booklets produced by HWCC. Where applicable, these also give details of train services. They are available from County Hall or from libraries and Tourist Information Centres. The County Council also provides a telephone information service on 0905 766800.

Services provided by the operators in the following list will enable you to complete every walk in this book.

DRM Coaches. Coach Garage, Bromyard. 0885 483219
George Young's Coaches. Holme Bungalow, Glebe Rd, Newent.
0531 821584

Lugg Valley Motors. 131 Etnam St, Leominster. 0568 612759
Midland Red West. Heron Lodge, London Rd, Worcester WR5 2NP.
0345 212 555
Morris's Coaches. Broadbridge House, Bromyard. 0885 482285
Newbury Coaches. Lower Rd Trading Estate, Ledbury. 0531 3483
Primrose Motors. Worcester Rd, Leominster. 0568 612271
Red and White. Bulwark Garage, Chepstow. 0291 622947 or 063 33 5118
Sargeant Brothers. Mill St, Kington. 0544 230481.
Smith's Motors. The Homend, Ledbury. 0531 2953.
Teme Valley Motors. The Garage, Leintwardine. 054 73 223.
Tudor Coaches. Water's Edge, Lower Rd, Ledbury. 0531 2073.
Yarranton Brothers. The Garage, Eardiston. 058 470 229.
Yeomans' Canyon Travel. Three Elms Trading Estate, Hereford.
0432 356201
British Rail 021 643 2711
National Express 021 622 4373

Rights Of Way

Like most English counties, Herefordshire has a dense network of footpaths, evolved over many generations. Sadly, however, this does not mean that access to the countryside is all that it should be. Paths are often difficult to follow, obstructed, or simply not there any more. In 1989 a survey by the Countryside Commission concluded that walkers in England and Wales have just a one in three chance of completing a two mile walk without encountering difficulties.

Each of the routes in this book has been walked during the last few months of 1991, and each was, at that time, passable. They have also been checked on the Definitive Footpath Maps. This is no guarantee, however, that you will not meet with obstructions, which may take the form of crops across the path, barbed wire, electric fences and so on. Paths are also subject to change or closure. If you need to check that any of these paths is still a right of way you can do so by consulting the Definitive Maps which are available for inspection by the public at Hereford City Library.

The law relating to footpaths was recently clarified in the Public Rights of Way Act 1990. The most important points, in the context of this book, are as follows:

A farmer may plough a cross-field path but he may not plant it, and he should reinstate both the line of the path and a reasonably convenient walking surface within fourteen days for the first disturbance in any cycle of cultivation, and within 24 hours for any subsequent disturbance. The path should be a minimum width of one metre, and maintained at that.

A farmer should not plough a field-edge path at all, and it should be maintained free of vegetation to a minimum width of one and a half metres.

A cross-field bridleway should be at least two metres in width, and a field-edge bridleway should be at least three metres.

The farmer or landowner is responsible for the maintenance of stiles and gates. This includes keeping them clear of encroaching vegetation.

If a landowner does not fulfil his responsibilities the relevant highway authority, in this case HWCC, is obliged to enforce the law. It should also provide signposts wherever a footpath starts from a metalled road.

In practice the above requirements are rarely met. Not all landowners take their responsibilities seriously and HWCC has many other calls on its resources. Nevertheless, the Council has confirmed that it has adopted the Countryside Commission's target of having the whole footpath network in good order by the year 2000. The Council can act only if it is aware of the problems; it is up to us to keep it informed. If you find a neglected or obstructed footpath please note the details, including the grid reference if possible, and inform:

The Rights of Way Officer
County Engineering and Planning Department
HWCC
County Hall
Spetchley Road
Worcester WR5 2NP.

A Brief History of Herefordshire

Herefordshire may be one of England's most peaceful counties today but it was not always so. The earliest settlers have left little to mark their passing but the Iron Age Celts made their presence felt on the landscape, as the many surviving hill-forts bear witness. As successive streams of invaders, first the Romans, then a variety of Germanic peoples, swept across England, the Celts were pushed ever westward. What is now Wales became their stronghold and Herefordshire inevitably became a battlefield. Nor did the county escape the Danish menace for these raiders used the River Severn to penetrate deep into England and Herefordshire suffered with the rest. The Welsh took advantage of this to step up their own activities and when England eventually grew more peaceful and united an attempt was made to subdue the Welsh, with Harold Godwinson campaigning along the border and introducing the Norman system of castle building.

After Harold's death at Hastings the Conqueror had his own solution to the 'Welsh problem' (an English problem, surely?) He parcelled out the Marches, as the border country was known, to his most ruthless and unruly henchmen, on the understanding that they could more or less carve out their own independent 'kingdoms' as long as they kept the Welsh in order. They set to with a will and Herefordshire knew little peace under these Marcher lords, the most powerful of whom were the Mortimers. When not waging war on the Welsh, or on the king, the barons were squabbling amongst themselves, and the county inevitably suffered. They consolidated their hold by covering the land with castles, about ninety of them altogether, built largely by slave labour, and from these they sallied forth to rape and plunder whenever the mood took them.

By the 1280s Edward I had defeated the Welsh in a major campaign and established a certain amount of control over the country. The power of the Marcher lords began to decline, although they survived until Henry VIII abolished the system in 1536. Small-scale border raids continued but the only major Welsh uprising was that of Owain Glyndwr in the early 1400s. The accession to the English throne of the Welshman Henry Tudor in 1485 finally brought peace, consolidated by Henry VIII's Act of Union in 1536. The Tudor peace lasted until the English Civil War of the 1640s when most of Herefordshire, with some notable exceptions, was for the king. The county saw a fair amount of action with numerous skirmishes and sieges, but no major battles took place; a fact possibly of little consolation to the county's inhabitants who inevitably paid the heavy price of bands of soldiers roaming the land.

After the Civil War Herefordshire was left in peace to develop its massive agricultural potential. Herefordshire cider and beef were famous all over the world and the county prospered. By an accident of geology it has few mineral deposits so industrialisation largely passed it by. Herefordshire remained an essentially rural county and, even today, it has but one city and five smallish market towns. Of these, only Leominster and Hereford itself have so far shown a propensity for truly ugly urban sprawl to any significant extent. The county has mostly escaped the motorway menace too, with just one short intrusion of the M50 near Ross. All of which is not to paint a picture of a rural idyll; the countryside is changing and under pressure. Jobs are in short supply. The depopulation of the land continues apace, while incomers flood in to change the face of rural villages.

Whatever the changes and problems, however, Herefordshire remains one of the least spoilt and most undiscovered of English counties. Enjoy it while you can.

A key to the symbols used in the maps

The route followed, showing direction

Roads and lanes

Railway

Major rivers

Lesser rivers and brooks

Parking   P

Building mentioned in text or helpful in route finding

Church

Castle, or site of castle

Earthworks, eg hill-fort, deserted village, etc.

Prehistoric burial chamber

Summit

Broad-leaved woodland

Plantation woodland, mainly coniferous

Acknowledgements

Thanks are due to:

David Griffin, former Editor of the *Worcester Evening News*, who gave me a start in this particular field by publishing the *Walkabout* series. Four of the walks in this book appeared in the *News*, in a different form, during 1991.

The staff of the Tourist Information Centre in Ledbury which must surely be the friendliest and most helpful TIC in England.

All the kind and friendly people of Herefordshire (and Wales) whom I have met on my travels; in particular all those country bus drivers who have enabled me to reach the remotest corners of the county. Overworked and underpaid, they remain unfailingly cheerful, and are generous with useful tips and local knowledge.

Peter, Carol and David for checking so many of the routes.

My family for their interest and encouragement.

Martin for his help in the final stages.

Location Map

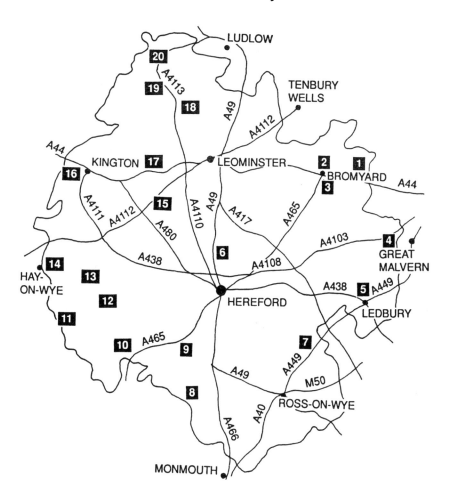

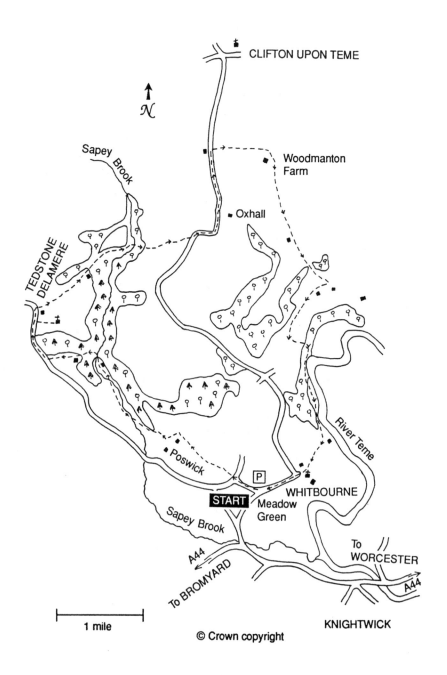

CLIFTON UPON TEME

N

Sapey Brook

Woodmanton Farm

Oxhall

TEDSTONE DELAMERE

River Teme

Poswick

P

START

WHITBOURNE

Meadow Green

Sapey Brook

A44

To BROMYARD

To WORCESTER

A44

1 mile

© Crown copyright

KNIGHTWICK

xiv

The Sapey Brook

This is one of the very best walks in eastern Herefordshire, with an unbeatable combination of hills and valleys, woods and water, traditional orchards and ancient houses, a wealth of wildlife and spectacular views. Marvellous at any time of year, it is perhaps best in spring when the fruit trees are in blossom, the wild flowers at their best, and Tedstone Delamere churchyard awash with daffodils. On the other hand, you may prefer late September when the hedges are laden with a feast of blackberries, hazel nuts and wild plums. Whatever the season, one thing you are almost assured of is solitude, for this is one of the least known areas of the county, most visitors being attracted to the nearby honeypots of Bringsty Common and Bromyard Downs.

Distance: 8½ miles
Maps: Landranger 149. Pathfinders SO 65/75(995) and SO 66/76 (973)
Start/Parking: At Meadow Green, ½ mile north of the A44 and 1 mile west of Knightwick (Worcestershire). GR 720567. Alternatively, park by Whitbourne church, ¼ mile north east. GR 725569.
Public transport: Midland Red West Worcester/Hereford services 419 and 420 call at Meadow Green.
Conditions: An easy walk on mainly good paths and quiet lanes but there are some muddy stretches, one very slightly awkward stile, a couple of overgrown patches and a number of slopes.
Refreshments: Nothing available *en route* but Meadow Green has a pub, a shop and the sort of old-fashioned Post Office which still sells sweets in glass jars.

MEADOW GREEN is not a village in its own right but actually part of Whitbourne, a quarter of a mile away. It has, in recent years, become the real village centre, providing a wide range of facilities. There are a few old houses but most are modern.

Walk along the main street to a junction where, on the other side of the Clifton road, there is a stile leading to a well-defined path across arable fields. There are very extensive views from here; on the left is Bringsty Common, immediately recognisable by the very distinctive clump of trees which crowns it, and beyond is the ridge of Bromyard Downs. Also on the left, but much closer, is Whitbourne Hall, a large mansion built in classical

Greek style in the 1860s for Edward Evans who had made his fortune in his family's vinegar and wine business in Worcester. To the right are the Worcestershire hills of Ankerdine, Berrow and Clifton, while straight ahead you can see Tedstone Delamere Court perched amidst conifers high on the top of a hill overlooking the Sapey Valley.

The path leads straight ahead across five fields to Poswick Lodge where you go between the farm buildings and through an old orchard to reach a rough track onto which you turn left. Both the Lodge and neighbouring Lower Poswick are examples (much-altered) of open-hall cruck houses, a type which belongs to the fourteenth century. For a closer look at Lower Poswick continue a little further along the track but, to continue the walk, leave the track as it bends sharply to the left. Go through the middle one of three gates into an orchard, following the right-hand hedge to a stile into a triangular field always full of rabbits and pheasants. Go downhill, bearing left along a ridge and through a gate into the valley of the Sapey Brook. Head upstream towards Tedstone, soon crossing the brook by a footbridge but continuing in the same direction.

Looking like the River Teme in miniature, the Sapey Brook follows a meandering, tree-lined course and has cut down through the soft red marls to form surprisingly high and steep banks in places. If you are lucky, you may see a grey wagtail, an active little bird with striking grey and yellow plumage. Look out, too, for the majestic buzzard which hunts in these parts and is one of the few raptors which is currently doing well in Britain.

On the east side of the valley woodland comes right down to the brook and its name, Limekiln Coppice, indicates its former usage. Lime used to be important for building purposes and was obtained by heating locally quarried limestone to very high temperatures in kilns. A constant supply of timber was required to fuel these so they were usually to be found in woodland, often coppiced to provide continual regrowth.

Cross another footbridge and continue along the brook, passing an idyllically situated cottage. The west side of the valley is now wooded too and this stretch of trees is known as Limekiln Covert. Cross a third footbridge to reach a broad forestry track, turn right to a staggered crossroads, then go left uphill. At a T-junction turn right then immediately left. Continue uphill, passing an old farmhouse, Pixhill, and going through an apple orchard to the lane.

Turn right to reach Tedstone Delamere. There is no real village, just the Court and church, with a small scattering of other houses some distance away. This is a common pattern in eastern Herefordshire where, so often, a church is found in the middle of a field with just one house for company. (See also Walks 2 and 3 where this also applies to Edvin Ralph, Edvin Loach and Stanford Bishop). Sometimes this is because a medieval village has disappeared but more often it is a result of an early pattern of settlement in which parishes usually covered a fairly large area consisting of scattered farms and cottages. The church was built either in the centre of the parish or adjoining the largest farmhouse or manor house.

Neither church nor court is especially distinguished in an architectural sense but their setting can not be faulted. The view, at its best in the late afternoon, extends right across Worcestershire to the distant Cotswolds. The Malvern Hills look particularly dramatic from this angle.

The church is of Norman origin but only a little remains from this period thanks to Victorian 'restoration'. It is dedicated to St James, the same martyr whose shrine at Compostella in Spain has been one of the most important centres of Christian pilgrimage for centuries.

Looking downhill, you may see a herd of red deer. They are, of course, farmed, but, nevertheless, they make a striking and welcome addition to the landscape.

Return to the lane, walk past the court, and turn down the 'No Through Road' on the right. After passing a group of cottages take a look through the deer-fence on the right — you can sometimes get good close-up views of the animals from here. Go through a gate on the left and follow the track past Line House Farm to a junction. Go straight on and continue in the same direction, ignoring all turnings, until you reach a large arable field. Go downhill to the right of it, keeping close to the hedge. Continue to a rather overgrown footbridge, cross the brook, and walk uphill through the trees. This is a good example of the dingle woodlands which are so characteristic of the Teme Valley and its hinterland where fast-flowing tributary streams carve out deep gorges known as dingles. The steep, inaccessible nature of these has preserved their natural cover of ancient woodland and they can be magical places, their green depths full of dense, tangled vegetation with luxuriant clusters of mosses and ferns more reminiscent of Wales and the far west than the Midlands. Here, a narrow stream has cut steeply down through the rock to join the Sapey Brook and, although it has run dry in recent years, prolonged heavy rain restores a series of small waterfalls along its course.

Emerge onto a lane, turn right and walk for a few yards to a bend. Go through a gate on the left and follow a path across a narrow field to two gates. Go through the left-hand one and follow the hedge to a lane. Turn left and continue for three quarters of a mile, entering Worcestershire as you pass Oxhall Farm. Reach Upper House where, a few yards further on, is a hidden stile opposite which gives onto a path leading along the right-hand side of a planted line of tall trees. Follow the path to the end of the trees, then turn right for ten yards to cross the ditch by means of some large stones set into the bottom. Take care as the sides of the ditch are slippery after rain. Continue across an arable field, bearing slightly left to go through a white gate, then turning right to Woodmanton Farm. Older than it looks, the farmhouse incorporates a medieval timber-framed chapel and is surrounded by the remains of a moat. A 'licence to crenellate' ie fortify, was granted in 1332 and a large semi-circular tower surviving in a corner of the moat probably dates from that time.

Walk through the farmyard, turning right between the last two barns and past a pond to reach a surfaced path running across a field which, dotted with scattered large trees, has the appearance of parkland. Continue along this path for three quarters of a mile to Ayngstree, passing to the left of two houses to go down a grassy path by the edge of a garden. Enter an arable field, continuing in the same direction, then turning left to go downhill through trees, re-entering Herefordshire as you do so. When you emerge from the trees there are unexpected and quite superb views which extend for many miles.

Worcestershire is to the left and Herefordshire to the right. The River Teme, which forms the boundary, is itself mostly invisible but the 300 ft high wooded cliffs which tower over its west bank mark its course towards Whitbourne. The panorama includes Berrow and Ankerdine, the Suckleys, the Malverns, the Cotswolds, the high ground around Bromyard and the dim and distant hills stretching to the Welsh border beyond. Immediately below, a number of farmhouses, some of them timber-framed, fit perfectly into this setting.

Follow the hedge down to a gate and turn right along the lane, continuing for half a mile until you see a footpath on the left which leads across an arable field into Scar Coppice and down to the Teme. Walk along the river for half a mile, looking out for an interesting old abandoned cottage half hidden on the left.

Herefordshire's second largest river, the Teme is shared with Powys, Shropshire and Worcestershire and is reasonably unpolluted, thus retaining much wildlife interest. Rich in fish and invertebrates, it supports birds such as dippers, wagtails and herons, as well as the more usual mallards and moorhens. Colourful dragonflies and damselflies hunt along this stretch in good numbers from spring to autumn, the iridescent banded agrion being particularly beautiful.

Follow the river to a lane by a pumping station and continue to Whitbourne. The first building of interest you come to is the church. Dating from 1180 it has been much altered since, especially during the course of 'restoration' in 1865. It still retains a medieval lych-gate with a lovely stone-tiled roof, under the rafters of which is stowed the old parish funeral bier. Inside the church are some relics of its Norman origins, including the font, crudely carved with The Lamb of God, the emblem of St John the Baptist to whom the building is dedicated. In a glass case on the north wall is a fifteenth century elaborately embroidered cloak, thought to have belonged to an early Bishop of Hereford. Hidden behind the ugly pulpit is a lovely modern window depicting St Francis with various birds and animals.

Next to the church stands Whitbourne Court, built on the moated site of a palace of the Bishops of Hereford. The palace was demolished to make way for the new building in the seventeenth century when it came into the hands of Colonel Birch who had been a noted Parliamentary leader in the Civil War. Whitbourne appears to have been one of the favourite palaces of many of the Bishops, two of whom were actually buried here, although no trace of their tombs remains today. One of them, Bishop Godwin, who died in 1633, wrote *The Man on the Moon*, an early piece of science fiction.

The village itself came into being partly through the Bishops' need for a work-force for the palace. During the Civil War the villagers remained staunchly Royalist and, on one occasion, armed with pitchforks and scythes, they tried to prevent a detachment of Roundheads from occupying the palace, but proved no match for the soldiers' cannon.

Opposite the church is the former rectory, originally a medieval house but largely rebuilt in Georgian red brick with Venetian windows. It is a beautiful house and there are several more of interest if you turn down the main street. One has unusual and ornate sixteenth century brick chimneys, and others date from the fourteenth century.

Finally, return to Meadow Green by crossing the bridge over Whitbourne Brook and walking along the lane for a quarter of a mile.

2

The Edvins

This is a lovely walk through the fertile farming country to the north of Bromyard, with good views of the surrounding hills, and two tiny villages which we will call Edvin Loach and Edvin Ralph. Maps, signposts and local usage, however, also offer Edvyn, Edwin and Edwyn, giving a total of eight permutations, an interesting survival of medieval inconsistencies in spelling. Originally known as Gedeven, the area was later split between two families, the Ralfs and the de Loges. The two estates became Gedeven Ralf and Gedeven de Loges, changing over the years through Gedefen and then Edefen to the present day Edvin (or Edwin etc). The transition from Ralf to Ralph, and de Loges to Loach was achieved with more consistency.

Distance: 7 miles
Maps: Landranger 149. Pathfinder SO 65/75 (995)
Start/Parking: There is a free car park in Bromyard just off the Tenbury road (B4214) signposted from the High Street. GR 653548
Public transport: Midland Red West Worcester/Hereford services 419 and 420 stop on Pump Street, just off High Street. Other services provided by DRM Coaches, Go Whittle, Bromyard Omnibus Company, Morris's Coaches and Yarrantons.
Conditions: Mostly good underfoot. One or two slopes but nothing that could be called a hill.
Refreshments: Nothing available *en route*. Plenty of choice in Bromyard. Appreciators of the ironic might enjoy the Chinese chippy near the car park with the wise but inappropriate name of Shun Fat!

BROMYARD is not only a convenient starting-point but is itself well worth exploration. An attractive and unpretentious little town, it gives few hints of its former importance when, in Saxon times, it was the third most important town in Herefordshire after Leominster and Hereford itself. Its church, referred to in a charter of AD840 as 'monasterium', which translates as 'minster' or 'great church', served an unusually large parish and was probably an important mission centre. The present church dates from the late twelfth century but it also contains some earlier Norman work, and many later alterations and additions. It was a favourite of the Bishops of Hereford who had a palace here, no trace of which remains today.

The Edvins

A market developed at the gateway to the Bishop's Palace and Bromyard became a commercial as well as an ecclesiastical centre. The street plan which was laid out at around this time is still clear today, with narrow streets running off on either side of the High Street and Broad Street.

Bromyard looked all set for a prosperous future but was particularly badly hit by the Black Death in 1348. It never really recovered and the first National Census in 1801 recorded a population of only 983. Poverty was

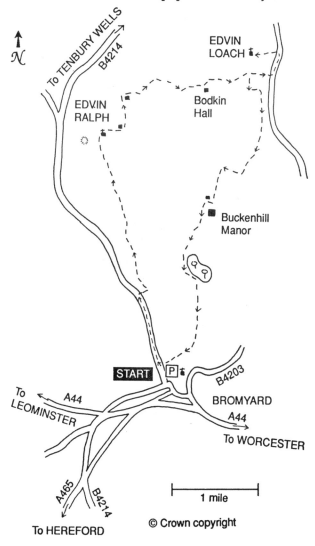

The Tower House, Bromyard

such that in the 1850s Bromyard's mortality rate was one of the highest in England. A short-lived spell as a railway town brought some revival and Bromyard also became known for its horse fairs until increased mechanisation cut the demand. More recently, light industry has been attracted and many new houses built. Bromyard is now a lively, flourishing community of about 2,500 with its own theatre, community hall and sports centre. A Folk Festival held every September attracts many visitors.

Walk north along the Tenbury road, passing a small industrial estate built on the site of the former railway station. Opened in 1878, the railway gave a slight but much-needed boost to Bromyard's economy but later fell victim to the Beeching Axe which descended on Herefordshire with more than usual severity. In the heyday of the railways the county had forty-three stations but today only four remain. After about half a mile pass between the remains of the old railway bridge then cross the River Frome. Just after this the road bends to the left and on the bend is a bridleway leading to Buckenhill Manor on the right. Go along here but after a few yards climb a stile on the left into a pasture. Follow the well-defined path as it leads past a garden then along the field-edge by a dry stream-bed fringed with alders, hawthorns, oaks, hazels and willows, many of them draped with a luxuriant growth of ivy.

Continue by the hedge through two more pastures. Both partridges and pheasants occur here and, in summer, there are usually speckled wood butterflies, indicating that the line of trees once formed part of a more extensive woodland. The path climbs slightly and there are good views over to Bromyard Downs.

Cross a lane, climbing a stile just to the right into a pasture dotted with oak and ash trees, and with good views to the east of an entirely unspoilt landscape of hills, woods, fields and hedgerows. Bear diagonally right across the field to a stile visible in the hedge below. Climb the stile and turn left along the hedge, noticing the beautiful white willows down to the right. Unlike most trees, the white willow is at its best in midsummer when the silvery sheen of its leaves makes a pleasant contrast to the uniform dark green summer foliage of other species.

Cross a footbridge and continue. As you reach the highest point of the field stop to admire the excellent views behind you. Climb a stile, then another after about 30 yards. Continue in the same direction but now to the left of the hedge. When you reach another stile climb this and walk through the trees, crossing a footbridge and two more stiles to reach a pasture. Walk up the field, keeping close to the hedge. At the top of the field the short, squat tower of Edvin Ralph church, topped with a tiny spire, comes into view. Go through a gate and cross a pasture to a footbridge. (If you have an OS map you will notice that the above directions do not exactly correspond with the map — this is due to a slight path change).

Cross the footbridge. Immediately in front of it is an unusual pollarded ash tree (a species not often subject to this technique) and to the left a holloway leads to a perfectly circular moat surrounded by trees and encircling an island of about 40 yards in diameter. Unlike many, the moat still holds water and moorhens breed here alongside the sheep and cattle which come to drink. (There is no official access to the moat which is slightly off the footpath). Cross the field to the church, climbing a stile in the west wall of the churchyard.

St Michael's church used to be the centre of the village and there are more earthworks visible just to the north of the moat which indicate where the village stood prior to depopulation, probably due to the Black Death. Another hollow in the field is thought to be the site of a monks' fish pond for there was a religious community here too. The later village developed a little to the north on the Tenbury road. The twelfth century church is simple and attractive and contains what is considered to be one of the most important collections of medieval effigies in Herefordshire. They used to lie in the chancel but have been unceremoniously dumped on the floor below the tower to make way for new choir stalls. They represent fourteenth century members of the Edefen family, including one Matilda de Edefen whom local tradition asserts was the victim of a quarrel over her between two rival suitors, one from Edvin Ralph, the other from Edvin Loach. She came upon them duelling, rushed between them and was pierced by both their swords. The men fought on to the death and all three were buried in the church.

On the wall, not far from the effigies, an old record of donations to the poor mentions a Mr Sharrott who "gave Six pounds to remain a Stock for the Poor for Ever". Six pounds may have gone further in Mr Sharrott's day but, even so, he must have been a considerable optimist!

Leave the churchyard by the main gate and turn right along the lane, continuing past Townsend Farm and Brickhouse Farm. There are some superb old pollarded oaks along here and good views across to Bromyard Downs. Go through a metal gate and continue along the lane as it becomes a bridleway running along the edge of a cornfield. When you reach a metal gate on the left which opens onto a tarmac drive go down here to Bodkin Hall. Turn left to go past the farm buildings. Just after the last one an overgrown path on the right leads faintly down to a footbridge over a stream, then uphill through an old orchard carpeted with wild flowers and alive with butterflies in the summer. Keep to an old hedge on the right, climb over a collapsed wooden gate and go across an arable field, passing to the right of a cottage. Continue across a pasture, noticing the castellated West Lodge of Saltmarshe Castle on the right. Built in the Victorian period, the castle itself was pulled down in 1955 and there is now a caravan park on the site.

Go through a gate to a junction of paths and walk downhill to the lane, turning left, then left again, to visit Edvin Loach's two churches. The old church of St Mary is in ruins; until quite recently it was overgrown but is now in the care of English Heritage who have tidied it up, added a gate and fenced parts off. Surrounded by closely-mown grass it has none of the romantic appeal of Avenbury (see Walk 3) but it does have some interesting herring-bone masonry and is partly constructed from huge blocks of tufa. This stone, also known as travertine, is formed from carbonates deposited by streams in some limestone areas. Although it has a spongy texture, seeming soft and porous, it is actually very durable. The stone was quarried locally, perhaps at Southstone Rock, just over the border in Worcestershire, and one of the biggest tufa deposits in Britain. The church was built in the eleventh century but the tower is a later addition, perhaps sixteenth century. Behind the church is a mound which probably represents some sort of early fortification.

The new church was built in Early English style and designed by Sir George Gilbert Scott, being completed about 1860. An old photograph displayed inside shows how the old church looked before it fell into decay; tiny and utterly charming as it nestles incongruously by the side of its newly-built supplanter, it has a little pointed roof topping its tower.

Admire the far-reaching views from this elevated churchyard then retrace your steps to the junction of paths, again entering the pasture and crossing it to a stile, half-hidden by a bend in the hedge. Climb over then turn left to follow the hedge down the field, turning right at the corner and continuing to the right of the hedge through two arable fields and a pasture. Cross a footbridge and gate into a field on the left and continue in the same direction down a pasture. Cross a footbridge and go uphill to the hedge. Turn right and walk to the corner of the pasture, going through a metal gate into another pasture and turning left to follow the hedge.

Continue until you reach a small farm building on the right and turn right behind it along a farm track with the walled garden of Buckenhill Manor to your left. The name means 'beech hill' and beeches still grow hereabouts. The house dates from about 1730. Notice an old wooden granary supported by staddle-stones. These were once widely used to prevent rats getting at precious grain stores, the rats being unable to negotiate the overhang.

Pass to the right of the house, going through a gate onto a farm track. Turn right along it. Shortly before reaching a white-painted cottage go to the left, climbing a stile by the corner of a wood and following the woodland edge. It is an unusual wood with coppiced ash and ancient, gnarled elders. Young cattle seek shelter from the sun in its shady recesses during the summer. When the wood ends go through a gate onto a farm track. Bromyard church is now in sight, perched on its hill ahead. On the left is a river, stay close to this through several fields (the path is obvious) until you see a hump-backed stone bridge on the right. Cross this and follow the path to the road just outside Bromyard. Turn left to return to the town.

3

The Frome Valley

The term 'rolling countryside' is much over-used but for once is justified. Indeed, it might have been invented specifically to describe the landscape south of Bromyard, especially to the west of the Frome Valley. Look back now and again as you follow the path south towards Avenbury Court and you will see why. These fertile, well-drained slopes mostly face south and west and must have been attractive to the earliest settlers; although only a little evidence has been found it is likely that this area was farmed in Neolithic times several thousand years ago. Today it is still farming country with a mix of pastoral and arable.

Distance: 7½ miles
Maps: Landranger 149. Pathfinder SO 65/75 (995)
Start/Parking: There is a free car park in Bromyard just off the Tenbury road (B4212) signposted from the High Street. GR 653548.
Public transport: Midland Red West Worcester/Hereford services 419 and 420 stop on Pump Street, just off High Street. Other services provided by DRM Coaches, Go Whittle, Bromyard Omnibus Company, Morris's Coaches and Yarrantons.
Conditions: Mostly good underfoot, with no steep slopes but lots of undulations. Some nettles, and one or two slightly awkward stiles which might be a problem for some elderly people.
Refreshments: Nothing available *en route*. Plenty of choice in Bromyard. The Old Penny Restaurant in the High Street does excellent afternoon teas, and lunches and dinners Wed-Sat. Loafers' Patisserie on Broad Street does the best value flapjacks in the Midlands!

IF this is your first visit to Bromyard it is well worth exploration before you start the walk. For some notes on the town see Walk 2 (The Edvins). From the junction of High Street and Broad Street walk along Pump Street, crossing the by-pass and continuing past the timber-framed Tower House where Charles I stayed in 1644. With its close-set framing and lozenge-decorated gables, this is one of the most impressive buildings in Bromyard.

Go past the hospital and down a rough lane, soon crossing a cattle grid to follow a farm track, with the River Frome meandering along its tree-lined course to your left. The second smallest of Herefordshire's seven rivers, the

12

The Frome Valley

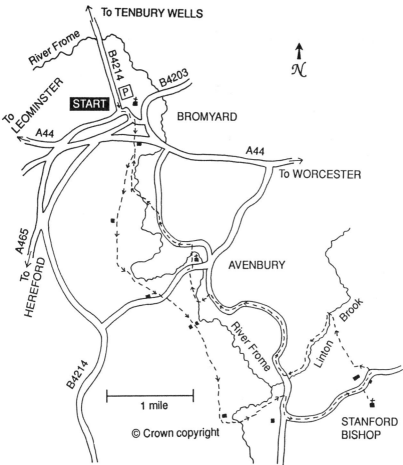

To TENBURY WELLS

River Frome

To LEOMINSTER

B4214

B4203

P

START

A44

To HEREFORD

A465

B4214

1 mile

© Crown copyright

BROMYARD

A44

To WORCESTER

N

AVENBURY

River Frome

Linton Brook

STANFORD BISHOP

Frome rises a few miles to the north near the Worcestershire border and flows south-west to join the Lugg near Hereford. Although only a minor river it has given its name to many settlements along its course including Canon Frome, Bishops Frome and Castle Frome.

On reaching a junction of three paths near Little Frome Farm keep left, then left again in front of the house. Walk up the left edge of a cornfield to go through a gate in the hedge. Bear diagonally left over a pasture, going through a gap in another hedge to pass between Avenbury Court on the right and a row of five oak trees on the left. Continue straight on to emerge onto a lane just in front of Avenbury Court. Cross the lane and walk down a pasture to enter a hopyard.

Known as hop-fields elsewhere in England, but always hopyards in

13

Herefordshire and Worcestershire, these have been part of the local scene for many centuries. Hops were not widely grown in England until the sixteenth century but in Herefordshire some seem to have been grown as early as the fourteenth century and there are constant references to hop kilns and hop poles in medieval documents. Hops need sheltered, well-drained but moisture-retentive soils; such conditions are easily provided in this part of Herefordshire. Each plant produces long shoots which are trained on a wire framework supported by poles. After harvesting, the hops are dried in kilns in oast-houses. Before mechanisation became widespread in the late 1940s hops were picked by hand and hordes of pickers would arrive from the Black Country and South Wales each season. Hop growing has declined in recent years and most oast-houses have been converted to private residences. It is still quite important in parts of Herefordshire, however, and production is concentrated in a triangle formed by Hereford, Ledbury and Bromyard.

Turn right, cross a footbridge and go uphill to Brookhouse Farm, passing to the right of the house to enter an arable field. Follow the hedge to the top of the field, turning left through a gate then shortly right through another gate. Continue through two fields, keeping close to the hedge. Stanford Bishop church now comes into view on a hill over to the left and so does an isolated stone building in a field, known as the Rumney Building. This looks like a field barn, and is used as such today, but it was once a school for girls, founded in 1731, rebuilt in 1826, and endowed by the local vicar. Continue to Upper Venn Farm and turn left along the farm track to the lane. Turn right then shortly left at a junction opposite the Rumney Building. Continue for just over half a mile, looking out for the easily missed turning on the right to Stanford Bishop church.

The church of St James the Great stands on a hill and commands extensive views in every direction — to Bromyard Downs, to the Malvern and Suckley Hills, and across the Frome Valley. The churchyard is circular, a shape indicative of great antiquity, especially when it is also in an elevated position like this one. In fact, it is believed that this was a place of religious significance well before Christianity came to Britain, a theory at least partially confirmed by the presence of a standing stone in the hedge by the gate.

A large yew tree in the churchyard is estimated to be 1,200 years old, predating the present church which mostly belongs to the thirteenth and fourteenth centuries, although it also incorporates some Norman work. Inside it is fairly plain but it contains an unusual treasure, the intriguing 'Augustine's chair'. St Augustine was sent from Rome about AD600 to introduce Roman-style Christianity to England. He became Archbishop of

Stanford Bishop Church

Canterbury and, in 603, attended a Synod somewhere in the west of the country, though the exact location is unknown. At the meeting he so alienated the Bishops by his arrogance that a distrust of the Roman church was established, nearly a thousand years before the actual split occurred.

In 1846 James Johnston, a student on a walking holiday, noticed an ancient chair in Stanford Bishop church. Though it interested him he went on his way thinking little more of it. Forty years later he returned and found the chair being used as a garden seat by the sexton. He bought it from him and, back home in Birmingham, his research convinced him that this was the chair used by Augustine in 603. His conclusions were partly based on its method of construction which seems to be that used by Roman carpenters at the time. The chair was later sent to Canterbury but was returned to Stanford Bishop for greater safety during the 1943 bombing raids. Further examination by experts has cast doubts on its provenance — they say it is simply not old enough. Whatever the truth, the chair is certainly very ancient and continues to be proudly displayed in the chancel.

Return to the lane and continue in the same direction. Pass a large house called The Hawkins then a black barn on the right. Just after this go through a gate on the left and cross the field to a second gate. Turn left, crossing a pasture to enter an old orchard through a gate which is about 50 yds to the right of the house. Go left to another gate and turn right along a farm track leading to two field gates. (These directions do not correspond to the OS map due to path changes by the owners of The Hawkins). Go through the left hand gate and follow the hedge down through several fields to Linton Brook, turning right through a gate just before descending gently to the brook. Cross a footbridge and turn left, following the lovely tree-lined brook to a lane. There are one or two awkward stiles along here but they will not present any problems for most people.

Turn right along the lane for about a mile then go left at Brookhouse Farm drive. Cross the River Frome and immediately turn right to follow the river then bear left to the hedge to reach a lane. Turn right then shortly left down a narrow path to the atmospheric ruins of twelfth century Avenbury church. The old churchyard is much overgrown with nettles so it's best not to wear shorts and, as the notice warns, you enter at your own risk! The path passes to the right of the tower, leaves the churchyard by a stile and crosses a footbridge opposite. Cross a small field to a lane, turn left and continue until you reach a footpath signposted on the left which crosses the Frome and follows its course back to Bromyard.

4

Cradley and Mathon

Immediately to the west of the Malverns is an area of wooded limestone hills, green valleys and beautiful 'black and white' villages. Rich and fertile, the land has been settled since the earliest times and has long supported a mixed farming economy based on cattle, sheep, corn, orchard fruits and hops. Mathon, in particular, used to be an important hop-growing area with its own specific variety which was much favoured locally. Hops are no longer of great importance to the local economy but some are still grown. Overshadowed by the neighbouring Malvern Hills, this part of the county is often overlooked with the result that, on a summer Sunday, when the Malverns are seething with visitors, you can explore these quiet lanes and footpaths without ever encountering another walker.

Distance: 7 miles (+ 2 miles if starting from Great Malvern)

Maps: Landranger 150. Pathfinder SO 64/74 (1018)

Start/Parking: Park in West Malvern, just below the open land of the hills, to the east of the B4232, near the church and schools. GR 764462.

Public transport: Newbury Coaches Ledbury/Malvern service 675. Otherwise walk across the hills from Great Malvern which has excellent bus and rail connections (see box on following page).

Conditions: Good underfoot, although some paths may be muddy after rain. There are some climbs but nothing strenuous. The paths are unusually well-signposted, well-maintained and easy to walk.

Refreshments: Cliffe Arms, Mathon. Post Office Stores, Cradley. A fair choice in West Malvern.

A LITTLE way to the north of West Malvern village centre the Cradley/Mathon road joins the B4232. From this junction walk down Croft Bank by the side of St James's and The Abbey Schools. Turn right along Croft Farm Drive and walk past four houses before turning right onto a bridleway. Go through a gate into a pasture with superb views up the valley to Storridge and Birchwood in Worcestershire. Cross three pastures on a well-defined track to reach Birches Farm.

Over on the other side of the valley is Cother Wood, a HNT reserve. There are no public footpaths in the wood but HNT members are able to explore it. A SSSI, Cother Wood is an ancient woodland which contains trees such as small-leaved lime and wild service; species which are generally quite rare in Britain but locally common along the Herefordshire/Worcestershire border. On the western slopes of the wood are areas of grassland with an interesting flora, including several varieties of orchid.

At Birches Farm pass to the left of the farmhouse via a complicated series

---

If you are starting from Great Malvern...

walk up St Annes Road (which leads off Belle Vue Terrace in the town centre, by the Angel Inn), going straight ahead when it bends left. Where the tarmac ends go forward and steadily uphill along a broad grassy track. When the track forks, go left, still ascending. Cross a well worn track and continue forward past an easily missed marker stone signed West Malvern.

Just over the highest point take the left fork and descend. Cross a firm track by the side of an old, and still working, gas lamp. Cross the grass opposite, go through a gate and down the hill into West Malvern. Reaching the B4232 your route lies opposite, down Croft Bank, signed to Cradley and Mathon. Now continue from the previous page.

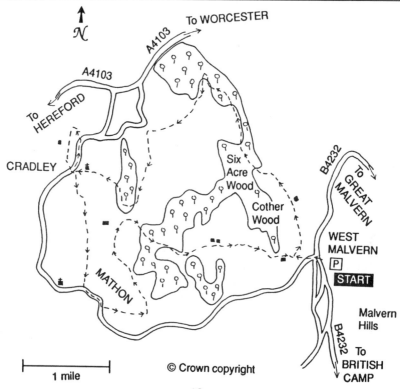

1 mile

© Crown copyright

of gates and fences and continue along the track in the same direction before turning left to cross a stream, following the field-edge to a gate straight ahead. Go through here and take a faint path leading diagonally right into Six Acre Wood, immediately north of Cother Wood. There are excellent views from here back to the Malverns.

Eight miles long, the Malvern ridge is composed of a mixture of rocks, including pre-Cambrian ones 620 million years old, some of the oldest and hardest in Britain. On the eastern, Worcestershire side the ridge rises with stark and startling abruptness from the Severn plain, but here, on the west, the slopes are gentler and more wooded, less dramatic perhaps, but more picturesque. The highest point is Worcestershire Beacon and from this peak southwards the county boundary runs more or less down the spine of the hills, physically marked in places by the Shire Ditch which was originally a boundary between the hunting territories of the Earl of Gloucester and the Bishop of Hereford.

Walk into Six Acre Wood, noticing some very fine old gnarled hawthorns lining the path and some beautiful ash trees hung with wild clematis. Go through a metal gate and continue through the wood. Arrive at a broad ride and go right, then right again at another junction after a few yards. Continue on the well-defined path along the edge of the wood for a while, then re-enter the trees before crossing a pasture then returning to the wood. Continue to a point just below an old quarry now reclaimed by nature. Turn left here, following an obvious path downhill. As the path leaves the trees there are good views, both to the Malverns and to tree-covered Cockshot Hill directly ahead.

Go downhill to a lane, turning right along it. Just before a junction take a footpath to Cradley, indicated on the left, and walk by the hedge along the edge of two pastures. There is woodland over to the right and soon a stream appears on the left. Continue by the side of the stream and eventually climb a stile into the wood. It is bright with flowers in the spring but August and September are the liveliest months when what seems like the entire squirrel population of Herefordshire is frantically collecting the hazel crop.

Ignoring a footpath on the left, continue through the trees along a path which is rich in flowers in spring and summer. Pink centaury and yellow St John's wort make a striking combination in July. From April to October several species of dragonfly hunt along here, including the spectacular blue, green and yellow southern hawker.

Climb a stile into a pasture, cross a stream and continue to Cradley, now visible ahead, emerging into a rough lane near to an impressive timber-framed and jettied building which is now the village hall but was formerly a boys' school. First built in the fifteenth century, it was extensively restored in 1674. Just beyond it is the church of St James. Most of it dates from about 1868 and was the design of Sir George Gilbert Scott, but the splendid tower of grey stone stained green and orange with lichens and lightly clothed with a Virginia creeper, was built around 1200 and incorporates a length of Anglo Saxon carved frieze in the north wall. There is a medieval lych-gate, attractive gardens and a shapely yew tree. Across the lane are two black and white cottages, over-restored but still pretty.

Inside the church you can see the timber-framed interior of the old tower and a font with an unusual and lovely decorated wooden top, made in 1722. An interesting painted notice of 1795 lays down the rules for bell-ringers and the penalties for breaking them.

Walk down the lane to a junction by the war memorial and turn right. There are a number of attractive houses along here; notice especially Clematis Cottage and the old Post Office. About 100 yds past the Post Office, at a bend in the lane, take a footpath on the left which goes along a driveway with Cradley Brook flowing between willows and alders to the right.

On the OS map the right of way goes along the driveway through the grounds of Wold Mill, but this has now been diverted. Shortly before reaching the Mill climb a stile on the left and follow the waymarked path by the side of a hedge to reach a lane. Turn right and walk to Brookside Cottage, opposite which, behind a parking place, is a half-hidden stile. Climb over and follow the path to a lane and turn left to return to the war memorial.

The Post Office, Cradley
20

Go right along a path signposted to Mathon, passing a long, white-painted house to reach a bend in the lane. Go through a gate on the right into an arable field. Bear left to the hedge and follow it up the field. Cross a farm track and continue in the same direction. Climb a stile, go straight ahead to a footbridge over Cradley Brook and continue to the lane, emerging near the green at Mathon.

The village is first mentioned in an Anglo-Saxon charter but there has been a settlement here for much longer than that. A little way to the south of the village, at South End Farm, is the site of the only known Bronze Age urn burial ground in Herefordshire. It was uncovered in the early years of this century when quarrying for sand was being carried out (Mathon is famous for its good quality sand and gravel). Bones and bronze spearheads were found in the urns, and these finds are now in Malvern Museum. More urns, along with stone battle-axes and pottery of a much later date were found to the east of the first site and are now displayed in Hereford Museum. The Bronze Age relics are thought to date back to around 2,000BC and the later pottery shows that the site was still in use 2,000 years later in the Iron Age and Roman periods.

To visit St John's church turn right along the village street. Built by the monks of Pershore Abbey, probably in the twelfth century, it contains some Norman windows and herringbone masonry. The fourteenth century tower is in the Perpendicular style and inside there is a very fine fourteenth century roof to the nave. In the churchyard are the remains of an ancient preaching cross and a thousand year old yew tree.

Retrace your steps to the village green and continue along the lane, passing the Cliffe Arms and a number of interesting houses. When you come to a stile and footpath sign on the left by a fast-flowing stream follow the stream across three pastures to reach a farm track. Turn left onto this, continuing for three quarters of a mile to Netherley Hall Farm where there is a junction of paths. Turn right, going up the slope and over a stile to enter the trees on Cockshot Hill. Follow the path through the wood which contains numerous wild cherry trees whose white blossom makes this a lovely place in the spring. Join a major track which soon leaves the trees to reveal good views of the Malvern Hills and also Rowburrow Wood on the right. Look out for buzzards which may sometimes be seen hunting here.

The track passes to the right of Highgrove and Bank Farms and continues downhill, then ascends slightly to a bend where there is a stile. Go over here and walk up along the edge of the trees then straight on over the pasture to join a farm track. Turn right along it for a short distance before taking a narrow path on the left which leads to a stile by some conifers. Pass through Croft Farm and return to your starting point by turning left up Croft Bank.

5

Oyster Hill

The lovely old town of Ledbury attracts its fair share of visitors in the summer but few take the opportunity to explore the surrounding countryside, even though Ledbury is at the centre of an excellent network of footpaths. To the south and west of the town the landscape is flattish with much arable farming, but to the north and east the foothills of the Malverns provide some very rewarding countryside. This walk takes you through orchards and over hills to the peaceful village of Old Colwall, then back again on a ridge walk through woodland.

Distance: 8 miles
Maps: Landrangers 149 and 150. Pathfinders SO 63/73 (1041) and SO 64/74 (1018)
Start/Parking: Ledbury town centre, where a car park behind St Katherine's Hospital is signposted from the High Street. GR 711377.
Public transport: Ledbury has a fair train service on the Worcester/Hereford line. Bus services are provided by DRM Coaches (476 Hereford) and Newbury Coaches (675 Malvern, 678 Gloucester). There are other, infrequent, local services, and a daily National Express coach (308 Aberdare/Birmingham).
Conditions: The paths are mostly excellent but some are very muddy after rain. A few slopes but nothing too strenuous.
Refreshments: Nothing available *en route* but plenty of choice in Ledbury.

L EDBURY'S recorded history began in AD720 when an Anglo-Saxon mission church, or minster, was founded. The town developed around the church, on land mostly owned by the Bishops of Hereford who had a palace here. In the 1120s Bishop de Capella, obviously hoping for commercial growth, superimposed a planned Norman pattern on the Saxon town, with a new larger marketplace. The Bishop's layout still partly survives, with many small alleyways leading off a very long main street, and the market is still held in the same place.

Ledbury prospered, becoming an important cloth-making and tanning centre. The wealth generated by these activities led to much of the town being rebuilt from about 1570 to 1630. Most of today's buildings date from this period, including the impressive Feathers Hotel and Ledbury Park, often said to be the finest timber-framed house in the county. However, prosperity later waned due to the appalling state of the roads, bad even for Herefordshire which was renowned for its poor roads. The turnpike trusts carried out improvements but Ledbury people rioted against the tolls which were imposed, some being sentenced to death as a result. In an effort to boost trade a canal was constructed but was soon replaced by railway lines linking the town with Gloucester, Hereford and Worcester. The Hereford/Worcester line still survives, making Ledbury one of the most easily accessible of Herefordshire towns.

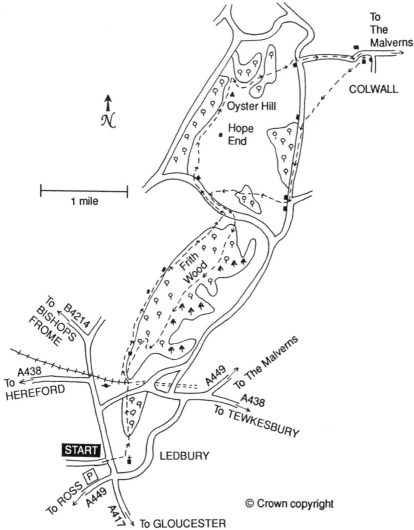

© Crown copyright

If you arrive by bus or car you can't miss the town centre. If you come by train simply walk along The Homend. The most prominent building in the centre is the seventeenth century, timber-framed Market House, supported by sixteen massive chestnut pillars. Walk behind it to find Church Lane with its beautiful, timber-framed, jettied houses. Walk along the lane to St Michael's church, built by the Normans in the twelfth century to replace the Saxon minster. It has been much added to since and contains many interesting memorials. It is one of only seven in the county to have a detached bell-tower, an impressive structure whose spire tops 200 ft. The church door is riddled with bullet-holes from a Civil War skirmish when Prince Rupert drove off a force of Roundheads. A sword from the battle is displayed inside.

Church Lane, Ledbury

From the churchyard turn left along the path by Bank Cottage to a road by a school. Walk up the steps ahead into Dog Hill Wood where snowdrops, anemones and bluebells flower successively throughout the spring. Go straight on through the wood to reach Knapp Lane. Walk along the footpath opposite which crosses the railway then bends to the left. Go into a field and turn right to follow the yellow arrows. (If you come by train and do not wish to explore the town you can join the walk here by turning right from the station and shortly right again onto a footpath leading uphill to this point). Cross a cottage garden to enter an orchard. Keeping to the right, follow the edge of the orchard, ignoring all paths into Frith Wood, and enjoying the far-reaching views. The impressive 30-arched viaduct on the left carries the railway across the River Leadon and was built in 1859-61, needing over one million bricks for its construction. Pass a converted oast-house, dropping down to join its driveway, and continuing to Frith Farm where you take a signposted path on the right, following the waymarks along the edge of the wood.

When the wood finishes turn left along a track to reach a wooden gate. There are superb views from here of the Malvern Hills, especially the 1115 ft high Herefordshire Beacon. The hill-fort which crowns its slopes is known as British Camp and is one of the finest in the country. It was built by Celtic people between 500 and 200BC and its huge ramparts enclose an area of 30 acres which would have been home to at least 2000 people. The hill-forts were important centres of population which developed from the need to combine an easily defended site with a good vantage point, and British Camp exemplifies this principle perfectly. Occupied for hundreds of years, the forts were, in the end, no match for the Romans, who sacked them all, forcibly resettling any survivors in the valleys.

Note a footpath on the right which is the return route for later, then turn left along the lane, continuing to a Victorian lodge where there is a sign for Hope End Hotel. To the left of this is a footpath which you follow over the hill, bearing left towards the trees, then straight on, looking down at the walled garden of Hope End, the childhood home of the poet Elizabeth Barrett Browning.

When the Barrett family moved here Elizabeth's father was not content with the house that existed and he replaced it with a sort of Moorish fantasy, complete with minarets. Unfortunately, the house was later destroyed, except for the stable-block which is now a hotel. Elizabeth was a child prodigy, writing poetry from an early age. She also loved to explore the countryside but a riding accident at 15 damaged her health permanently. Disaster followed on disaster as her mother and then her brother died, her father lost his money, and they moved to Wimpole Street in London where her possessive parent kept her closely confined. She found an ardent admirer, however, in fellow poet Robert Browning, and when she was forty they married secretly, escaping to Italy. Elizabeth's father never forgave her but she enjoyed a brief period of happiness before her premature death at 55.

Go over a stile by the edge of the trees and on to the 700 ft summit of Oyster Hill. The view encompasses the Welsh mountains to the west, the Shropshire hills to the north, and the Malverns, Suckleys and Cotswolds to the east.

Park Farm, Colwall

Head downhill between two converging areas of woodland to a red earth track. Turn right to follow it uphill a little way then go left across a wide grass verge to a stile into a sheep pasture. Follow the path across fields and through two patches of woodland, eventually passing a cottage to emerge into a lane. Turn right to a junction and then left to Colwall church.

Since the building of the railway in 1861 Colwall has developed into a large village which spreads eastwards to merge with the Malvern towns. All that, however, begins three quarters of a mile away from the church and the cluster of houses making up the old village which has remained peaceful and unspoilt. St James's church dates mainly from the thirteenth and fourteenth centuries and has a beautiful collar-beam roof inside. By the east gate of the churchyard stands a sixteenth century timber-framed ale house. A gathering at a church ale house was in many ways the equivalent of today's church fête, an innocent enough occasion, but the Puritans disapproved and by the mid-seventeenth century most ale houses had become schools or, like this one, alms houses. Recently restored, it is open to the public on summer Sundays, but you may look through its diamond-latticed windows at any time. Church and ale house together make a pleasing group in a beautiful setting, completed by Park Farm just over the lane. Dating from 1630, this is built on the site of an earlier house which the Bishops of Hereford used as a hunting lodge on visits to Malvern Chase.

26

From the rear of the church car park take a footpath which goes diagonally right to a clump of trees by the far corner of the field. Continue along the field-edge for a few yards then cross the brook by a footbridge and bear very slightly right to the stile visible in the hedge ahead. Continue in the same direction over the next field to reach a lane just to the left of a house. Turn left, walking for half a mile to a junction by two houses. Turn right between them, following the path along the edge of fields and through a short stretch of woodland to the lane near Hope End.

Turn left and walk to the footpath noted earlier, going uphill to Frith Wood which, although a Forestry Commission woodland, is not all conifers but retains a good mix of native, broad-leaved species with a good butterfly population and varied birdlife. Look out especially for jays, green woodpeckers and buzzards, which may be seen anywhere around the Malvern Hills. An obvious path into the wood leads through the trees to a stile. At this point you are confronted with a choice of three paths. Take the middle one which gently climbs to lead you along the top of the ridge, with superb views to either side. As it gradually descends again the trees shut out the view but are themselves very lovely, especially in the autumn. Eventually the path begins to descend more steeply and soon brings you to a crossroads (or a T-junction if you discount the very faint path ahead). Turn right here, following the path as it curves back and then down to join a wide forestry track. Turn left and continue to a stile and gate where you have a choice. Just before the stile a track on the left leads into the wood — just continue along it to leave the wood. Alternatively, you can continue along the main forestry track, passing through the garden of Frith Wood House from where you can go downhill to the station or turn left for Knapp Lane and/or the town centre.

6

The Lugg Valley

Herefordshire's central plain lacks the strong scenic appeal of the surrounding hills but it has its own subtle charm, to which this walk serves as a gentle introduction. The river Lugg rises in Radnor Forest in Wales, flowing SE to join the Wye near Hereford. From Leominster southwards the river's flood-plain is broad, flat and fertile, but annual winter floods have preserved much of it from arable farming and the meadows are still largely given over to grazing, the river itself still bordered by ancient pollarded willows. Close to Hereford as it is, this is now commuter country, but there are still good numbers of interesting old houses, and the area is rich in history and folklore as well as wildlife. Flat it may be, but the hills are never far away and there are some excellent views to be had.

Distance: 5 miles
Maps: Landranger 149. Pathfinder SO 44/54 (1017)
Start/Parking: By Sutton St Nicholas church, 4 miles N of Hereford, 1¼ miles NW of the A465 Hereford/Bromyard road. GR 534454.
Public transport: Lugg Valley Motors Hereford/Leominster service 426. MRW Worcester/Hereford services 419 and 420 stop at Withington Marsh and Sutton Marsh on the A465 (1¼ miles).
Conditions: An easy walk with one gentle climb. The paths are not all obvious, and the riverside meadows may be damp, or flooded, in winter.
Refreshments: Golden Cross Inn at Sutton St Nicholas. A Mini Market and two pubs at Marden.

START from the Norman church in Sutton St Nicholas, simple and attractive with its old wooden porch roofed with mossy stone tiles. The village itself is largely modern but still contains many older houses, with brick, timber and stone all contributing to the overall picture. Walk to the left along the main street, going straight on at the crossroads and turning left down a narrow lane at the second crossroads. Very soon turn right over a stile, crossing two fields, an orchard and a garden to reach a lane. There are two gates ahead; go through the left-hand one into a pasture and cross to a stile. On the right is Sutton St Michael, now incorporated into its larger neighbour, but formerly a village in its own right until abandoned in the Middle Ages. Some bumps and hollows still remain in the field but they are

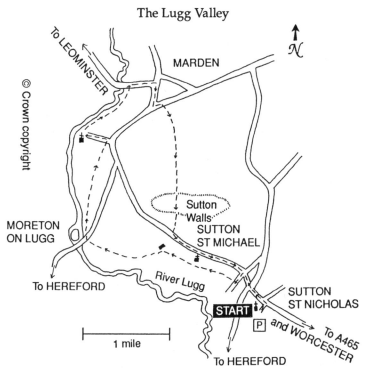

very slight and visible only in good light. A little Norman church still stands and contains two interesting fonts; one is the original, decorated with four carved lions, the other is an elegant and rare seventeenth century example.

Cross a second pasture, noticing the slight hill which now comes fully into view on the right, its lower slopes given over to crops, its top covered by trees. Though unimpressive-looking it is the site of an important hill-fort built by Iron Age people in the first century BC. It is of the univallate type; that is, it has just one rampart, which follows the contours of the hill. Its name, Sutton Walls, derives from the Latin *vallum*, a rampart. Sutton Walls was occupied until attacked by the Romans. When the site was excavated in 1948 heaps of skeletons were found, most of them with evidence of injuries, some decapitated — a graphic reminder of the fate of those who dared resist the power of Rome. Some occupation continued after this time but the fort slowly fell into disuse and decay. No evidence has ever been found of any later Dark Age or Anglo-Saxon occupation but tradition insists that it was the site of the palace of Offa, Saxon king of Mercia in the eighth century.

Cross an arable field towards Freens Court Farm ahead, going through a gate to the left of the farm and then left through double gates, following a

Ancient pollarded willows in the Lugg Valley near Moreton Bridge;
River Lugg in flood

track across the field to a footbridge. As you cross this notice the remains of a moat on the right. Go straight ahead for a few yards then bear right to follow a long, straight, dry ditch to a stile. Continue in the same direction across two more fields to reach a lane by an old stone bridge over the River Lugg. Cross to another footpath which leads along the river-bank. Herons, mute swans, grey wagtails and kingfishers may all be seen along here and in the winter the floods attract waders and wildfowl. The river is bordered by old pollarded willows which look good in any season. Pollarding is a traditional management system in which trees are lopped every few years, at a height of eight to twelve feet, and allowed to grow again to produce successive crops of timber, a technique which can substantially prolong a tree's life. Several types of tree respond well to this method but generally speaking only willows in lowland river valleys are regularly pollarded nowadays.

There is an anglers' path along the river to Marden church but the actual right of way soon veers away from the river, bearing right at first, then going straight on across the fields to reach a lane near a junction. Turn left to Marden church, beautifully situated by the river, but some distance from the village. The explanation for this is provided by what may be either history or legend; in AD793 King Offa invited King Ethelbert of East Anglia to his palace at Sutton Walls to discuss a marriage between Ethelbert and Offa's

30

daughter. It occurred to Offa, however, that perhaps this was not such a good idea for it would serve to increase Ethelbert's already considerable power, perhaps at the expense of his own. Offa, therefore, had the prospective bridegroom murdered and his body buried by the river. When the burial was followed by a powerful light filling the night sky, Offa, fearing divine retribution, hastily gave a tenth of his property to the Church and dashed off to Rome on a pilgrimage. The Pope told him to build a church on the site of Ethelbert's grave and this was done, although the present church is a later replacement. Ethelbert's body was later moved to Hereford and enshrined in a great new cathedral of stone, replacing the former wooden structure.

How much truth there is in the story no one will ever know, but Marden is certainly a place of legend. Another strong local tradition tells how one of the church bells fell into the river and was carried to the bottom by a mermaid. It was eventually hauled out by a team of cattle, with the mermaid asleep inside. A careless shout awoke her and she dived under again, taking the bell with her. Neither bell nor mermaid has been seen since but the bell has been heard ringing underwater on many occasions.

From the north corner of the churchyard a footpath leads along the edge of a garden where some very inquisitive and friendly chickens scratch about freely as chickens should, and a herd of white geese stands guard. The path continues across meadows to Marden's seventeenth century bridge, sticking closely to the river except where the Lugg loops away to the west. The alders which grow along here seed prolifically in the autumn, attracting flocks of goldfinches.

Turn right to Marden village then right again at a junction and left at the next but one (Paradise Green), soon turning right onto a footpath which runs straight ahead to the summit of Sutton Walls. The path is mainly to the right of a hedge but at one point you need to climb a stile to the other side, crossing back again at the first opportunity.

Enter the trees and continue to the flat, bare top of the hill where it is possible to walk right round the perimeter (about one mile). The views are good in the winter when not obscured by the trees, otherwise there is little to see as most of the interior has been destroyed by quarrying, although a large part of the rampart survives. The sheer size of the site, 28 acres, is impressive, however, causing you to wonder how Iron Age hill-forts can ever have been considered to be merely defensive positions. It is only quite recently that a re-evaluation of their role has established the fact that these were centres of population, fortified villages where people lived and worked, not just sites to which they retreated when danger threatened.

Continue along a major track leading downhill to Sutton St Michael and turn left to return to Sutton St Nicholas.

7

Marcle Hill

Much Marcle, close to the Gloucestershire border, is at the centre of a fertile plain which used to belong to the hop and the Hereford cattle, but is now mostly given over to cornfields. The deep, rich soils have been responsible for much prosperity, reflected in the numerous fine farmhouses and manor houses which dot the landscape, some of them dating back to the fifteenth century, others to later periods of agricultural expansion such as the 'Great Rebuild' of 1570-1640. The long ridge of Marcle Hill provides an opportunity to walk on higher ground from which there are excellent views over several counties, and Much Marcle itself, though only a small village, is of considerable interest.

Distance: 8½ miles
Maps: Landranger 149. Pathfinder SO 63/73 (1041)
Start/Parking: By the church in Much Marcle, just off the A449 Ledbury to Ross road. GR 657328.
Public transport: Extremely limited but best attempted from Ledbury. Contact Ledbury TIC for details (Tel. 0531 6147) or the following operators: Smith's Motors, Tudor Coaches, George Young's Coaches.
Conditions: Easy walking, good underfoot, with just two gentle climbs. Except for the stretch from Noggin to Nuttal the paths are well-maintained and waymarked.
Refreshments: Nothing available *en route*. Much Marcle has the Walwyn Arms and the General Stores (on the A449) and Westons' Cider (see map).

THE name Marcle derives from the Old English *mearcleah* meaning a boundary wood, although there is very little woodland to be found today. The prefix distinguishes it from its smaller neighbour, Little Marcle, three miles to the north. The large and attractive church, dedicated to St Bartholomew, is not especially remarkable in itself but it contains one of the finest collections of effigies in Herefordshire, the most interesting of which is a painted, wooden carving of a man hewn from a solid block of oak 6 ft 4in long. Less than 100 such wooden figures exist in the whole country, and Herefordshire has only one other, at Clifford. It is thought to represent Walter de Helyon who lived at the nearby house Hellens around 1357.

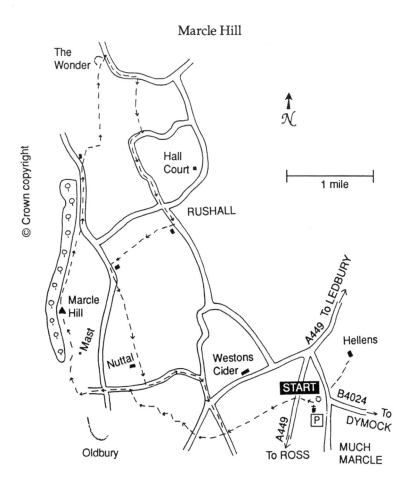

In the churchyard is a massive yew tree, over 30 ft round and estimated to be about 1,500 years old. If so, it pre-dates the church by some 750 years and was in existence soon after the Romans abandoned these shores, around five centuries before England became one kingdom! Its branches, supported by a timber framework, spread for 70 ft and its hollow trunk contains seating for seven or eight people.

To the north of the church, and shared between several gardens, is a twelfth century motte and bailey site known as Mortimer's Castle. The large motte, 170 ft across and 20 ft high, still survives, as do parts of the bailey, the ditches and the outer enclosures — but these have been much altered by the activities of generations of cottage gardeners. A stone keep which once surmounted the motte was dismantled after the castle fell into disuse, the stones being used to build the church tower in the fifteenth century. The Mortimers came from Normandy at the Conquest, were granted extensive lands on the borders, and remained a powerful presence in the area for centuries.

Leave the churchyard by the rear gate, crossing a driveway to a footpath and bearing slightly right over a field to the road. Cross over and bear left along a waymarked path through three fields to reach a lane. Already there are good views behind to the Malverns, the Cotswolds and May Hill near the Forest of Dean.

Cross to another footpath, bearing right across fields to a lane. Walk up the farm track opposite to a cottage, climb a stile on the right and follow the arrows to the left along the hedge to another stile. Turn right along the hedge, following it to a third stile. Turn right along a gravel drive to the lane and go left. At a crossroads continue straight on uphill, with a tall radio mast on your right. Strictly speaking, this is Ridge Hill and Marcle Hill is its northern continuation, but the whole ridge is more often known as either Marcle Hill or Marcle Ridge.

Continue up and over the top, going a little way downhill to where a footpath crosses the track. To the left is Oldbury Camp, an Iron Age hill fort, 17½ acres in extent. There is little to see as the defences have mostly been ploughed out but the rampart is still visible on the steep west slope.

Turn right along the top of Marcle Hill, soon crossing a stile to walk between a hedge and a narrow belt of woodland. Although the summit reaches only 760 ft there are great views of the Welsh mountains and the midland hills, with the slender spire of Ross-on-Wye church prominent to the south. In April the path is lined with the beautiful, delicate flowers of the wild daffodil which, though rare throughout most of Britain, grows in great profusion in parts of Herefordshire, Worcestershire and especially Gloucestershire. In the 1930s special excursion trains used to bring Londoners in their thousands to see the daffodils a few miles further south around Newent. Daffodil numbers inevitably suffered as the visitors, not content merely to look, gathered armfuls to take home with them.

When the footpath ends by a car park continue in much the same direction along a lane. Join a track to the right of a house called Hooper's Oak, soon turning right downhill then left at a junction. Where the track meets the road there is an exposed rock face on the left, about 15 ft high. It doesn't look very dramatic but it is actually the result of a massive landslip and for the past 500 years has been known as The Wonder. The historian Camden described the event — "... a hill which they call Marcley Hill, in the year 1575, roused itself, as it were, out of sleep, and for three days together, shoving its prodigious body forwards with a horrible roaring noise, and overturning all that stood in its way, advanced itself, to the astonishment of all beholders, to a higher station". It overthrew trees, hedges and a chapel before coming to rest in its present position. Other earthquakes were recorded in Hereford in 1661 and 1975 and there are occasional tremors along a fault line running south-west from the Malverns.

Turn right along the lane then shortly right onto a footpath (there is no sign so look out for a stile by a gate). Walk along the field-edge then bear right past some trees, continuing across the next field, passing under the power lines to a gap in the hedge. Continue to a stile and go straight on over a pasture. Notice the magnificent timber-framed house Hall Court over to the left. Built in 1608 it has been very little altered since.

View towards the Malverns from Nuttal

Continue to a lane, emerging opposite a converted barn. Turn right then left at the junction, continuing for just over half a mile to Cockyard Farm, turning right onto a grassy track then going left to a gate and up steps to an arable field. Walk by the hedge, shortly climbing a stile to continue by the right of the hedge to a lane. Turn left past Noggin Farm to a bend in the lane, going left into the field and bearing left across it, passing close to a solitary oak tree to reach a stile. Continue in the same direction, keeping close to the hedge. Pass Nuttal Farm, going through two gates into a field and straight ahead to a stile to the lane. Turn left to a T-junction, turn right and continue to a crossroads. Go straight on, taking the first footpath on the left, which is the one by which you originally left Much Marcle. Retrace your steps to the village.

Hellens, one of England's oldest family houses

Once back you may like to visit Hellens which is open on certain days through the summer (Tel. 053-184 668) and which is reached by a footpath opposite the church. Probably named after the de Helyon family, this house is one of England's oldest family houses, dating in part from 1292. It was much altered in Tudor and Jacobean times, being reconstructed in brick with stone mullioned windows. Architecturally superb, it has numerous historical associations — with the Black Prince, Mary Tudor and many others. In 1326 it achieved notoriety when Roger Mortimer fell in love with Edward II's Queen and installed her here, protected by his private army.

The grounds contain fine terraced gardens, a cider mill and an unusual octagonal brick dovecote of 1641.

8

Garway

This is a remote, little-known area on the Welsh border which, centuries ago, formed part of a region called Archenfield by the English and Erging by the Welsh, where Welsh custom prevailed for over 200 years after the Conquest. The Welsh influence remains strong today and the grey stone houses belong more to Wales than to England, a fact underlined by the many Welsh place-names. Garway is in a beautiful setting above the Monnow valley, and Garway Hill rises to nearly 1,200 ft — no great height really, yet this exhilarating walk has a decidedly upland feel to it and offers some spectacular views .

Distance: 6½ miles
Maps: Landranger 161. Pathfinder SO 42/52 (1064)
Start/Parking: On Garway Common, just east of Garway village. GR466227.
Public transport: Midland Red West services 412, 413 and 414 from Hereford.
Conditions: A moderately strenuous walk with one or two short climbs but nothing serious. Mostly good underfoot but some mud in winter. Paths and stiles mostly well-maintained.
Refreshments: The Moon Inn, Garway Common.

GARWAY COMMON consists of a pub and a few houses scattered haphazardly on 23 acres of grassland with wooded areas and numerous small ponds. Walk along a lane opposite the phone box until it bends sharply left, at which point you go through a gate on the right and follow the hedge down two fields. Emerge at a lane and turn right, soon passing between the old stone buildings of Garway Court. Note the barn with narrow slit openings, so typical of this area. Garway's name derives from the Welsh Gaer-wy, meaning a camp by water, the site of which was on the land now occupied by Garway Court, overlooking the River Monnow (Afon Mynwy) below, which now forms the border between England and Wales.

Soon after passing the Court you come to a sharp right bend where you go through a gate into the field on the left. Go diagonally left to where the hedge ends then follow a line of trees down to a gate to the lane. Cross to a footpath opposite and go straight on over three fields then turn right along

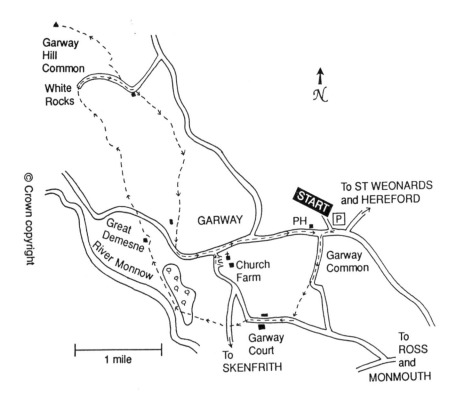

© Crown copyright

a wide tree-lined path above the Monnow. On your right the sheltered, west-facing Cockshoot Wood has a rich ground cover of a variety of ferns.

At the end of the wood go through a gate and follow the farm track across two fields towards Great Demesne Farm. Just before reaching it cross a stile on your right then walk towards the stone barn, looking for a stile on the left into the farmyard. Go forward to another stile then turn right onto the farm drive. The path bears left away from the drive to a stile near the far corner of the field (but as you have to duck under barbed wire here you may prefer to go along the drive instead). Opposite the stile a gate opens into a pasture and a farm track leads along the edge of three fields, eventually crossing a brook and going straight ahead over a rise to a gate. Continue straight on for a few yards then turn right along a major track, following it past farmhouses to a lane at White Rocks, one of the scattered hamlets which constitute the parish of Garway.

Turn right along the lane with the bracken-covered slopes of Garway Hill Common to your left and some wonderful views of the Welsh hills to your right. Pass several houses then start looking out for a stile on the left, sited several feet above the lane. Climb the stile into a pasture and follow the hedge uphill, going through a gate onto the open land of the Common.

There are several paths and it is well worth climbing to the summit, from which there are marvellous views on a clear day. A small herd of wild ponies roams the hill and you may see some fallow deer downhill to the north west where there is a deer park attached to Kentchurch Court, the home of the Scudamore family, and originally a fourteenth century castle before it was rebuilt by Nash around 1800.

Return to the lane and continue to a sharp left bend by White Rocks Cottage where there is a stile into a pasture. Go straight downhill, crossing a footbridge and stile and turning right over another stile into a large pasture. Follow the left-hand hedge until just over halfway up the field then go diagonally right to the far corner to enter the next field. Follow the right-hand hedge to a stile to an arable field and go diagonally across to the far corner, through a gate, and along the left-hand hedge. After passing a house you will see a drive on the right but stay on the path until it joins the drive. Continue to a lane, turning left into Garway village. Below is the church of St Michael and, next to it, Church Farm.

Turn right then left to the church, which dates from 1180 when Garway was granted to the Knights Templar, an Order founded by nine French knights in 1113 with the aim of protecting pilgrims in the Holy Land. Estates in England provided an income for this work and the Templars founded a preceptory (estate) at Garway consisting of the church and adjoining farm. Excavations have revealed the foundations of a round nave which was rebuilt in its present form in the fifteenth century. The round nave was the preferred style of the Knights who modelled their churches on the Holy Sepulchre in Jerusalem. Apart from the foundations, only the splendid chancel arch survives of the original nave. The massive thirteenth century tower was formerly detached from the church and served as a refuge in times of trouble. It was connected to it by a passage in the seventeenth century and seems to have been used as a prison on subsequent occasions.

Predictably perhaps, the warrior monks failed to live up to their high ideals and the Templars were dissolved in 1308. Garway was given to a similar Order, the Knights Hospitallers, who maintained ownership until the Dissolution. It was they who were responsible for replacing the round nave.

From the churchyard you can glimpse a circular stone dovecote at the farm but for a closer look you should ask permission of the farmer. It is a remarkable structure with walls 4 ft thick and 666 nesting places. It was built, or more likely, rebuilt, by the Hospitallers — an inscription over the entrance records that Brother Richard built it in 1326. This is considered to have been a rebuilding as it is representative of the very earliest type of dovecote found in England, the Norman columbarium, exactly similar to those built by the Romans who were the first to keep doves in this way. It is certainly the oldest dovecote in Herefordshire and one of the oldest and finest in all England.

Return to the lane and turn right through Garway to return to Garway Common.

9

Kilpeck

For many people the highlight of this walk will be the superb Norman church with its exuberant carvings; a mixture of the grotesque, the comic and the erotic, and including what John Julius Norwich has described as "a sheila-na-gig (or ancient fertility figure) of quite glorious obscenity". If that isn't enough to tempt you then the landscape itself should do the trick. This is still mixed farming country where the handsome red-brown Hereford cattle graze alongside sheep, horses, goats, geese and donkeys. With its rounded hills and abundance of woods and ancient hedges this is a remarkably unspoilt and remote-seeming area, despite its relative closeness to Hereford.

Distance: 5½ miles
Maps: Landrangers 149 and 161. Pathfinders SO 42/52 (1064) and SO 43/53 (1040)
Start/Parking: By Kilpeck church. GR446305.
Public transport: Midland Red West service 413 from Hereford (infrequent). Regular services to the Kilpeck turn at Wormbridge (¾mile) by Red and White 20 and Yeomans' 440/442 Hereford to Abergavenny/Newport.
Conditions: The terrain itself presents no difficulties though you should expect a little mud in winter. However, the overwhelming majority of the footpaths in this part of Herefordshire have been neglected, obstructed or lost altogether. All the paths which make up this particular walk have been checked on the definitive maps and they are all still rights of way. Furthermore, they were all passable, with care, in the winter of 1991. You will find, however, that you have occasionally to climb fences rather than stiles, that the local farmers do tend to be over-enthusiastic in their use of barbed wire, and that a stream has to be crossed on stepping stones. None of these obstacles will present great difficulties to the average walker but it is as well to be prepared. HWCC has been informed and it is possible that the problem will have been resolved by the time this book appears in print.
Refreshments: The Red Lion, Kilpeck.

T HE little Norman church at Kilpeck is the most famous in Hereford-shire and one of the most remarkable in the country. It stands on an ancient site, the raised, almost circular churchyard being typical of Celtic religious sites and the name Kilpeck is Celtic too. The Celts, however,

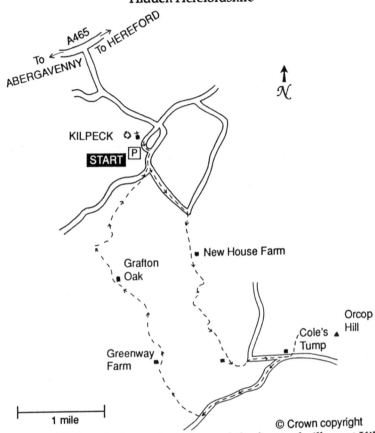

To ABERGAVENNY

A465

To HEREFORD

N

KILPECK

START P

New House Farm

Grafton Oak

Orcop Hill

Cole's Tump

Greenway Farm

1 mile

© Crown copyright

gave ground before the Saxon invaders and the first real village at Kilpeck was a fortified Saxon enclave in what was then Wales. The earthworks of this deserted village are still visible today close to the church. More prominent, however, are the remains of a castle built in the eleventh century by William FitzNorman. The motte rises nearly 30 ft above the bottom of the surrounding ditch and some fragments of the stone shell keep are still standing. King John was entertained here in 1211 and 1212 but the castle later fell into disuse and was finally destroyed by Cromwell's forces in 1645.

Kilpeck church, built around 1140, is almost pure Norman, consisting of a nave, chancel and semi-circular apse. What makes it so memorable is the mass of carving which represents perhaps the finest surviving achievement of the so-called Herefordshire School of craftsmen which flourished in the twelfth century and whose work is found all over the county, and in neighbouring ones too. There are intricate carvings all round the main door and a decorated corbel table runs along each wall. Of over seventy sculp-

42

The carved doorway to Kilpeck Church

tures in the corbel table, only two have any religious significance; the others are representations of animals, mythical beasts and humans, including some images which are disturbing, others which are erotic. A few are missing and it is thought that the delicate sensibilities of the Victorians were offended by what they saw here and, in an act of gross vandalism, these priceless works were destroyed. On the west wall are two projecting sculptures which resemble the figureheads of Viking longboats and, indeed, many of the motifs indicate that both Saxon and Viking influences were still part of English artistic life in the twelfth century. Inside there are more carvings, this time eminently suitable ones of saints, on the chancel arch. Notice also the massive font and an unusual stoup, both of which pre-date the church itself.

Once you've admired everything, and identified the *sheila-na-gig*, walk along the village street to a junction by the Red Lion and turn right, shortly forking left at a second junction. The lane leads steeply up to a T-junction where you turn right along a 'No Through Road' to New House Farm. Go straight on through the yard, passing through a gate into a pasture. Walk across, keeping close to the right-hand hedge. At the end of the field go through the right-hand gate and turn right. Walk round the field-edge until you come to a gate opening onto an obvious track, opposite to where you entered the field on the far side. Walk along the track, soon climbing a stile into a pasture, just to the left of a wood. Cross the pasture, keeping to the left, and shortly joining a track to a farm. Go past the farm buildings, turning left along a winding drive to meet the lane at a junction.

Go straight on towards Orcop Hill, nearly 1,000 ft high. The bare slope, crowned by a group of six trees, looks like the summit but is, in fact, an eminence known as Cole's Tump; the real summit is hidden from view. The tump is dotted with flat-topped, rectangular earthworks known as pillow mounds, constructed to facilitate the breeding of rabbits. This might seem a surprising idea to those of us who know anything about present-day rabbits; however, the modern rabbit is a very different animal from its medieval counterpart. The rabbit was introduced into England from Iberia by the Normans, as a source of food. A delicate animal, which had difficulty in burrowing into hard ground, it struggled to survive in England's cool climate. The less compacted soil of the specially constructed mounds made digging easier. It was only gradually that the rabbit adapted to become the hardy, robust animal we know today.

Reach a junction where there is a new house. A path just beyond the house will enable you to have a closer look at the tump if you wish. Otherwise, turn sharply right along the lane, soon passing through a cluster of houses. Not far beyond these is a bend, to the left of which stands a stone cottage with an attached barn. Just before reaching this look out for metal gates on both sides of the lane. Go through the pair on the right, walking along the right-hand field-edge then through a gap in the hedge. Bear left to a gateway in the middle of the next hedge and go straight on across another field, climbing a fence to join a farm track. Walk towards the farm but just before reaching the barns turn right over a stile then left, following the right-hand fence down the field. Climb over a gate and descend diagonally left to a brook, aiming for a point where a hedge on the other side comes down to it. Climb a gate and cross the brook with the aid of some stepping stones then walk up the hedge for a few yards to a gate into a pasture. Go straight across this and the next one. The brook on your right flows through a lovely, tree-lined valley and has a number of miniature waterfalls along its length.

Go diagonally left across a third field to join a green lane which passes the house Grafton Oak to reach a surfaced farm track. Turn right and gradually descend to cross the brook then immediately turn right over a stile into a small field. Follow the right-hand hedge then bear left to climb a fence to the right of a row of conifers. Keeping to the right of a stream, walk through the trees, soon crossing a footbridge and going straight on along a green lane. Where it joins tarmac climb a stile on the right into a field and go diagonally across to the far left corner, crossing a footbridge and stile into another field. Follow the left-hand hedge across two fields then go past a house and continue along the hedge to a gate to the lane. Turn right into Kilpeck.

10

The Dulas Brook and the River Dore

A lovely walk along two contrasting waterways which, though geographically close, are, in other respects, very different. The Dulas, with its miniature waterfalls, tree-lined banks, and steep-sided, sheep-grazed valley, has a very Welsh feel about it. The Dore, on the other hand, typifies the English side of Herefordshire's dual personality as it flows placidly along the twelve miles of the Golden Valley, bordered by fertile lowland pastures, orchards and, increasingly, arable fields. But why Golden? Well, to the Welsh the river was simply dwr (water), which, to the Normans, became d'or, a name which the English both retained, as Dore, and translated, as Golden.

Distance: 9 miles
Maps: Landranger 149. Pathfinders SO 22/32 (1063) and SO 23/33(1039)
Start/Parking: In Ewyas Harold village centre, GR388287.
Public transport: Yeomans' Hereford/Abbey Dore service 440. Red and White Hereford/Newport service 20 stops at Pontrilas (1 mile).
Conditions: Mostly good underfoot but a little mud in winter. There is some climbing but none of it strenuous.
Refreshments: Shops and two pubs in Ewyas Harold. The Neville Arms at Abbey Dore. Café/shop at Abbey Dore Court Gardens, open April-October.

EWYAS HAROLD, at the southern end of the Golden Valley, is a largish village with a fair amount of modern sprawl, but is redeemed by its attractive centre and its splendid common. The derivation of its name is uncertain, but Ewyas is either 'the place of the yew trees' or 'the place of the sheep'. Harold is not, as may be supposed, King Harold of Hastings fame, but an obscure nephew of Edward the Confessor. King Harold did, however, spend some time here, both before Hastings and, according to legend, after. The story goes that he survived the battle, and his injured body was removed by his mistress Edith Swansneck, with the help of monks from Waltham Abbey. Taken to the border country near Ewyas, he regained his health and became a hermit, devoting himself to a life of prayer. It's an appealing story, and could be true, especially as it seems there was a one-eyed hermit living in the Golden Valley in the late eleventh century. Perhaps, however, that in itself was enough to suggest the story of Harold's

Hidden Herefordshire

To HEREFORD, HAY and BRECON B4347

River Dore

Newcourt
Farm

N

BACTON

Riverdale

Dulas Brook

Hollingwood
Farm

Upper
Cefn

ABBEY
DORE

Abbey Dore
Court

River Dore

DULAS

Dulas Brook

Ewyas Harold
Common

P

EWYAS
HAROLD

START

1 mile

To PONTRILAS,
HEREFORD and
MONMOUTH
(and A465)

© Crown copyright

46

survival to an English nation struggling to maintain its identity under Norman domination.

The village is divided by the Dulas Brook, to the west of which stands a large, tree-covered mound which is all that remains of one of the most important border castles, built by the Norman Osbern Pentecost in about 1050 — it is not always realised that the Norman Conquest was under way well before 1066 thanks to the Confessor's habit of granting English lands to his Norman friends. The castle was destroyed and rebuilt more than once, but was refortified for the last time against Glyndwr in the early 1400s.

Across the brook stands the thirteenth century church whose tower has a clasping stair turret, an unusual feature in the borders. Walk round the churchyard and past some new bungalows to climb a stile into a field, walking up to the top left corner. Turn left along a track which skirts the common. At Weaver's Place pass in front of the house and through the garden, continuing in the same direction to Prince's Place where you go through the gate then immediately left through another onto a wide path which leads to a stone cottage. Turn left and shortly go through a gate onto the common.

This is the quintessential common, with thinly-scattered stone cottages nestling on its bracken-covered slopes. Kestrels hunt overhead, silver birches grow here and there, and the gorse seems to flower every month of the year. There are many paths and some wonderful views, especially of the Black Mountains.

Walk to the right and join a major path by a ruined wind pump. Turn right then left at the next three junctions. At the top of the common turn right to reach a concrete track then turn left onto a lane and go straight on, ignoring two turnings.

Pass Hollingwood Farm then turn left down a narrow lane which soon descends steeply to a ford and a footbridge over Dulas Brook, then on to the road. Turn right for a few yards and, just beyond a garage, go through a very large gate into the lovely valley of the Dulas Brook. Follow the brook closely for over half a mile to a footbridge. Cross over and bear slightly right up a steepish field until Upper Cefn Farm comes into view on the right. Don't turn towards it but carry straight on uphill to meet the end of a sunken track leading to the farm. Go through a gate opposite and walk diagonally left across a pasture. Climb a low fence to the lane and go left.

In less than half a mile you pass a wood on the right. At the far end of it go through a gate and follow the woodland edge, continuing in the same direction when an unfenced area of woodland joins it. Walk through the trees then go through a gate to a field on the right. Walk across the middle of it and pass through two gates to follow the left-hand hedge. Go through two more gates to a farm track where there are two gates on the left. Go through the second one and follow a track to a gate at the far right corner of the field. Don't go through the gate but turn left to follow the hedge, passing a cottage and a pond before reaching a major track. Turn left to St Faith's church at Bacton, a small, grey building of the characteristic border type, which was recently used in the film of the late Bruce Chatwin's book *On the Black Hill*.

Inside is a monument to Blanche Parry who was born at nearby Newcourt Farm and spent her life in service to Elizabeth I, becoming Chief Gentlewoman of the Privy Chamber. When she died in 1589 she was buried in London but her heart was returned to rest at Bacton. The memorial shows Blanche kneeling before the Queen in what is thought, aptly enough, to be a secular version of the earlier medieval motif of a worshipper kneeling before the Virgin Mary. Blanche served the Queen all her life and must have been her closest confidante; if anybody ever knew the truth about Elizabeth and the young men who clamoured for her favour then it must surely have been Blanche Parry. She is also mentioned on the stone benefaction tablet which hangs in the porch, and an embroidered altar cloth displayed inside is said to be her work.

Leave the churchyard and turn left downhill then left at the junction with the B4347. Just before you reach the bridge over the River Dore the course of the old Golden Valley railway is clear either side of the road, near the entrance to Newcourt Farm. The railway was opened in 1881 from Pontrilas to Dorstone, and later extended to Hay. Sadly, it never prospered and never managed even to own more than one or two items of rolling stock. It was closed down in stages, finally grinding to a complete halt in 1957.

At Newcourt Farm only a little remains of the childhood home of Blanche Parry, incorporated in the present building. Behind it stands a motte and bailey earthwork which indicates the site of an earlier fortified house, probably abandoned in the fourteenth century. (*For a closer look, there is a footpath to the farm along the right-hand edge of the wood*).

Cross the river and turn right at the first junction. At a sharp left bend go right past Riverdale, a rather forbidding-looking building — and no wonder, for this was once a Victorian workhouse, although now converted into modern homes. Go through a gate into a field and follow a farm track then bear right away from it when you see a stile ahead. The path is waymarked and the stiles are easy to spot. Just keep gradually edging closer to the river until you are sticking closely to its bank. When it later meanders away you go straight on to the lane. Turn left past Abbey Dore Court and very soon right along a signposted path. Go through a kissing gate and shortly left along the river. Go over a footbridge and cross two fields to reach Abbey Dore.

This Cistercian monastery was founded by French monks in 1147 and rebuilt 1175-1220. At its height it was immensely rich, holding seventeen farms in the Golden Valley and in Breconshire. Abbey Dore wool commanded one of the highest prices on the market. After the Dissolution the Abbey was more or less abandoned, even being used, at one stage, as a cowshed. In 1633 Lord Scudamore, with the aid of the renowned local architect and craftsman John Abel, embarked on a restoration programme, turning the Abbey into a parish church.

Do explore the interior, which is magnificent, then leave by the lych-gate. Opposite is a footpath which bears slightly right to the top of a field. Climb a fence and go straight ahead up the hill to another fence. Don't cross it but turn left and walk to a gate onto the common. Any one of the many paths will take you back down to Ewyas Harold but it's well worth spending time exploring the common first.

11

Hatterrall Hill

This is an exhilarating walk which introduces you to the darker side of Herefordshire in the shape of the easternmost ridge of the Mynyddoedd Duon, the Black Mountains, a little bit of Wales leaning over into England. In fact, the border runs along the top of the ridge before turning east to meet the River Monnow, and the Celtic heritage is still very strong throughout the area. Although the Normans established their usual political and military domination, in the valley at least, and built a substantial castle at Longtown, then known as Ewias Lacy, they never really made this area their own. Even after the borders were sharply defined in the reign of Henry VIII it remained more Welsh than English. The parishes were under the jurisdiction of the Welsh church until 1858 and Welsh was the language of the people until the early nineteenth century.

Distance: 7 miles
Maps: Landranger 161. Pathfinder SO 22/32 (1063). Outdoor Leisure 13
Start/Parking: Longtown, where there is a layby near the Post Office GR325287
Public transport: Yeomans' Hereford/Abergavenny service 442, Tuesdays only — just one return journey but the timing is perfect for the walk.
Conditions: This is not real wilderness, that lies further west. Nevertheless, for much of the year it is wise to be equipped for the worst weather England and Wales can throw at you. Even in summer the mist can descend without warning and it can be very cold. The Black Mountains can, and do, live up to their name; treat them with respect. There is one steep, pathless descent which requires proper boots and there is one potentially very muddy farmyard; otherwise, conditions underfoot are generally good.
Refreshments: The Crown Inn, Wheelers' shop and the Post Office Stores, all in Longtown. The Cornewall Arms at Clodock.

L ONGTOWN is a village of simple, grey stone cottages sheltering in the lee of the mountains. Walk north along the main street to the castle, of which a great deal more survives than the usual mound. A wooden castle was probably built here by Gilbert de Lacy in the mid twelfth century, and replaced by a more permanent stone building by Walter de Lacy, Sheriff of Herefordshire from 1216 to 1231. Much of the fabric is substantially complete, including what is thought to be the earliest round keep in

England. There is some suggestion that the castle stands on the site of a Roman fort, though there is no proof of this. Longtown castle belonged to various families after the de Lacys, notably the Despencers, the Beauchamps and the Nevilles; but they all lived elsewhere and it was mostly left to decay, except for a brief period when, like most border castles, it was re-fortified against the threat from Glyndwr in 1403.

Return to the Post Office and walk a little way south to a 'No Through Road' on the right. Go along here for a short distance until, after crossing the Olchon

© Crown copyright

LONGTOWN

START

P

To HEREFORD

Olchon Brook

N

Offa's Dyke Path

Pont Hendre

CLODOCK

Hatterrall Hill

River Monnow

To ABERGAVENNY

1 mile

Brook, you climb a stile on the right. Follow the brook round to a gate then go over the next field to a stile. Cross another field, aiming for a point near the far corner, jump a slight ditch and continue to the farm in the far right corner. Turn left through the farmyard and straight on along a concrete track into a field. Walk up here, keeping close to the right-hand hedge, and continuing into a second field. At the top of this climb a fence and bear left across the next field to a gate giving on to a fenced track. Follow this up onto the open slopes of Hatterrall Hill, go straight on for a few yards and then diagonally left to join an obvious path which you can see curving round the shoulder of the hill above and to the left.

At the top join a wide bridleway and head south. This is Offa's Dyke Path

51

The castle at Longtown

which runs for 168 miles between Prestatyn and Chepstow. Offa was king of Mercia from AD757 to 796 and built the long earthwork which bears his name in order to define his border with the Welsh. Even today eighty-one miles of the dyke are still clearly defined and it is surprising how often it coincides with the present border. The path follows the dyke for long stretches but, in places, diverts from it in favour of more scenic or more practical routes. Here on Hatterrall Hill it is a well-walked, obvious path so you can't go wrong as you stride south, one foot in England, the other in Wales. In fine weather the views are stunning, especially to the west where, immediately below, is the green and friendly-looking Vale of Ewyas, hemmed in by range after range of frowning mountains.

After about a mile you pass an old quarry where the remains of a stone shelter make a good place to have lunch, providing some respite from the vicious winds which so often blow up here. From the quarry it is another mile or so to a signpost indicating a footpath on the left to Hengastell (Oldcastle in English). The path runs through bracken and is barely discernible though it is supposed to go diagonally left. The descent is steep so pick the best way down. At the bottom a narrow path runs along by a tall hedge. Turn left along this path which soon becomes wider and goes between stunted hazels clothed in lichens. Pass two ruined farms then a small larch plantation. Go through a gate into a fenced area, at the other side of which are three gates. Go through the middle one and straight ahead into a field then across to the far corner where you pass through a gate, turn right and walk downhill for a few yards before turning right through another gate and continuing in the same direction only on the other side of the hedge.

Continue past a farm and on along a concrete drive which eventually becomes tarmac and leads past a second farm to reach the road. A footpath directly opposite crosses a small field, goes diagonally right across a second, over a footbridge and straight on across two more fields to reach the road by the Cornewall Arms at Clodock. Next to the pub is the church and it is likely that the first thing you will notice about it is how immensely crowded the churchyard is with hundreds of old headstones. Beautifully carved and delicately toned with the different greens of lichens and mosses they look marvellous. It is very rare for so many headstones to be preserved in this way, and even here a few have been used as stone stiles, but the vast majority have never been disturbed.

The church itself is an interesting one and was founded in AD520, although the present building is twelfth century and was restored in 1916-19. It is the only church in the world dedicated to St Clydawg, and this is the original name of the village, Clodock being an Anglicisation. Clydawg was a prince of Ewias, a saintly man who worked as a missionary, but he must have had more worldly interests too for, in the year 520, he was murdered by a rival in love. Legend says that as the oxcart carried his body to its funeral the oxen suddenly refused to continue when they came to a ford over the river. So Clydawg was buried there, next to the Monnow, and as people came to worship on the site a church was established and a small village grew up around it.

There is much of interest inside for this small village church is a treasure house of very fine woodwork installed in the 1600s. Also displayed inside is an ancient memorial slab, inscribed in Latin, which was dug up during the 1916-19 restoration. It commemorates the unnamed wife of a man called Guindda and is thought to date back to between 750 and 850.

Two stone tablets on the wall record a High Court decision of 1805 concerning a disagreement over tithes. The resulting payments are listed and include entries such as "Two Pence for every Barren Cow".

At the rear of the churchyard a path leads along the Monnow, then across three fields. Notice the large, tree-covered mound at Pont Hendre over on the left, surrounded by some smaller earthworks. This is the site of the original castle of Ewias Lacy. After it was taken by the Welsh under Prince Hywel in 1146 it was replaced by a stronger castle at what is now Longtown. The path veers away from the river in the third field and goes past the farm, keeping to the right of it, to reach a road. Turn right to return to Longtown.

12

Vowchurch Common

Herefordshire has many commons, but this is a term which is often misunderstood. Some people confuse them with village greens, while others assume that a common implies unrestricted public use. In fact, commons vary in their legal status and rights of access, and Vowchurch Common is an example of the privately-owned variety. Such a common is owned by an individual (or a company) but local people have certain traditional rights. Although public footpaths usually cross private commons this confers no right of access to the surrounding land, although, in practice, there is rarely much objection to considerate public use. Vowchurch Common is criss-crossed with an intriguing network of paths, many of them hidden, almost secret, with ancient green lanes forming leafy tunnels between fields. Perhaps the best way to explore it is just to wander at will, letting serendipity be your guide. This walk, therefore, serves merely as an introduction to the possibilities, and also ventures beyond the common to include some of the surrounding highlights.

Distance: 6 miles
Maps: Landranger 149. Pathfinder SO 23/33 (1039)
Start/Parking: Opposite the church at Vowchurch. GR 362365
Public transport: Red and White Hereford/Brecon service 39.
Conditions: An easy walk with little in the way of climbing. Some mud in winter.
Refreshments: There is a hotel at Vowchurch but it may not welcome muddy boots!

AT VOWCHURCH the multi-dedicated church (a total of fifteen saints, virgins and martyrs are named) forms part of an attractive group with the old stone bridge over the Dore and the timber-framed former rectory. Small though the Norman church is, it contains some impressive timberwork, including huge oak pillars, each simply a chamfered tree trunk. These were added in the fifteenth century, possibly to provide support as the roof has such a profusion of timbers that the walls may have been under considerable stress. Also interesting is a screen carved with the figures of Adam and Eve and the forbidden fruit, which, in this case, seems to be a pear rather than the conventional apple.

Continue down the lane from Vowchurch and in less than a quarter of a mile you come to Turnastone, which also has a small Norman church. Why

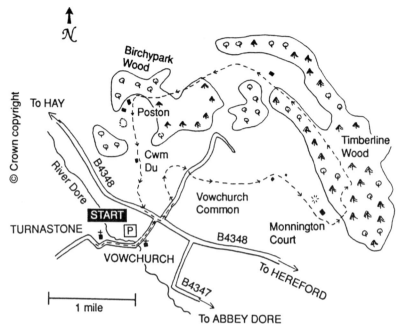

should two churches be built so close together? A local legend claims to answer not only this, but also to explain the meaning of the villages' names. There were two sisters who wished to establish a church but could not agree on the exact site. They quarrelled and each decided to build her own, one petulantly announcing "I vow I will build my church before you turn a stone of yours". In fact, Vowchurch comes from the old English Fow-chirche, meaning grey or mottled (and identical in meaning to the Scots Falkirk), while Turnastone means a settlement enclosed by a thorn hedge.

Near the church is a perfectly preserved village garage, a brick cottage with old-fashioned petrol pumps in its garden. On the cottage wall is a large Raleigh cycling advertisement, a survivor of the 1930s when cycling was at the peak of its popularity.

Walk back to Vowchurch and up to the main road. Cross to a steep lane opposite which leads to Vowchurch Common. When it bends to the right take a track on the left by the side of a white-painted house.

The track soon becomes a green lane before dwindling to a narrow path. When it emerges by a couple of cottages you turn right to reach a lane then cross to a green lane almost opposite. After three quarters of a mile you reach a junction. Turn right and shortly enter a field, pass a ruined cottage and walk along a holloway by the right-hand hedge. Soon after passing two trees

Turnastone village garage, with its old petrol pump

the holloway becomes a wide, muddy track and you cross a stone slab bridge into another field on the left. Go straight on towards Monnington Court Farm. As you approach it you will notice a distinct motte and bailey castle site, surrounded by a circular moat. Monnington Court is believed to be where the Welsh rebel prince Owain Glyndwr spent the last years of his life, in the early 1400s; in hiding after his campaigns against the English had failed to maintain their early success. The house (not the present one which is much later) belonged to his daughter and son-in-law.

Pass the farm buildings and the house to reach a lane and turn right for a few yards then climb a broken gate on the left and walk up the field into Timberline Wood which, like much of Herefordshire, belongs to the Prudential. It is managed for timber and for shooting. The waymarked path bends left then right to a T-junction. Turn left but very soon go right where the yellow arrow indicates, then left onto the bridleway (blue arrows).

Walk through the trees then along the woodland edge, continuing in the same direction when the wood ends and eventually passing to the left of an abandoned farm. Continue along the edge of arable fields to a junction and go straight on, soon entering Birchypark Wood. Walk along the edge of the trees then keep to the right across a bracken-covered, triangular clearing and enter the plantation ahead.

The path soon swings right and becomes a broad track. Ignore a footpath on the right and go left along the bridleway onto open land. Pass a tennis court then follow the arrows left past Poston Lodge Farm and on past beautiful Poston House, just south of which you will notice earthworks which mark the site of an Iron Age fort covering four acres. Excavations have revealed that it continued to be occupied throughout the Roman period.

Go through a metal gate and walk left along the line of the fence until you notice a pile of boulders to your right. Descend a steep coombe to Cwm Du Cottage. Climb a stile into the garden, turn left into an overgrown fold yard and then right into a field. Go straight down the field to another. Follow the right-hand hedge to its corner then go diagonally right to the far corner of the field, through a gate, and then diagonally left to reach the road. Turn left to return to Vowchurch.

13

Merbach Hill

Although this walk begins in the gentle Golden Valley it soon turns into an exhilarating, breezy climb to the 1,045 ft summit of Merbach Hill which offers sharply contrasting views; on one side the grandeur of the Black Mountains, on the other the vast flatness of the Wye Valley and the Herefordshire plain stretching away to meet the hills of western Worcestershire. Below Merbach Hill is Bredwardine, made famous by Francis Kilvert, and on top of Dorstone Hill is Arthur's Stone, the only Neolithic burial chamber in Herefordshire. Part of our route follows the Wye Valley Walk, a 107 mile waymarked path between Chepstow and Rhayader.

Distance: 7½ miles
Maps: Landranger 148. Pathfinder SO 24/34 (1016)
Start/Parking: The centre of Dorstone village. GR 313417.
Public transport: Red and White Hereford/Brecon service 39.
Conditions: Some steep slopes and an exposed hill top. The paths are mostly good but Finestreet Dingle can be extremely muddy for much of the year.
Refreshments: The Pandy Inn and The Stores at Dorstone. The Red Lion Hotel at Bredwardine.

ORSTONE sits snugly at the head of the Golden Valley, sheltered by the Black Mountains to the west and Merbach Hill to the north. The old village is clustered round the triangular green on which there is an unusual sundial made from the remains of the old village cross. Behind the village hall is a 30 ft motte which was the site of Dorstone's Norman castle. No masonry remains but the castle was still in existence in 1645 when Charles I and his army are recorded to have gathered here.

Walk down the 'No Through Road' which leads to the church of St Faith. Tradition links this with Richard de Brito, one of the four knights responsible for the murder of Thomas à Becket in 1170. De Brito is supposed to have spent fifteen years in exile in Palestine in expiation for his crime, and then on his return, sought sanctuary in Dorstone where he founded the church. However, an inscription stone discovered when the church was being restored seems to indicate that it was built in 1256 by John de Brito, probably Richard's nephew.

Take a path on the left which leads round the churchyard to the road.

Merbach Hill

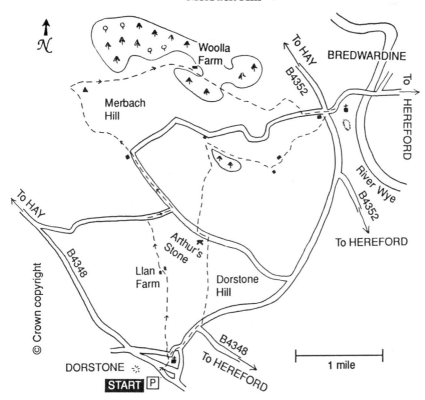

Cross to a playing field, walk along the right-hand edge then bear left to a stile and bear slightly left across a narrow field to a footbridge. Cross the old railway and walk to the far left corner of a field. Cross an overgrown track and climb a stile to a pasture. Cross to the far left corner and join a lane. Turn left then right through Llan Farm onto a track which goes steadily uphill to a lane. A couple of obstructed footpaths make a bit of lane-walking necessary here so turn right to a junction and then left until the lane bends sharply right by a stone house. Climb a stile onto the grassy slopes of Merbach Hill and follow the left-hand hedge before eventually bearing right towards two gnarled hawthorn trees. Continue uphill, passing through a small gate to reach the trig point. On a clear day the views are enormous and it is claimed that eleven counties can be seen.

Walk a few yards west of the trig point and you should see a narrow path threading down through the bracken to join a wide bridleway. This is well used by riders but some of the tracks you see will belong to the wild ponies which are found on this hill. Turn right then very soon fork left where a waymark indicates the Wye Valley Walk. The path leads through the bracken to a sharp right bend where you go straight on through a gate and cross two fields, then walk along the edge of a wood and past a black barn to reach open pasture. Go downhill to Woolla Farm and continue along the track, going through a plantation then across a pasture. A farm comes into view ahead and soon after a lesser track intersects the main one, coming across from a gate on the right. At this point turn left along a dip between the farm and a tree-dotted ridge which ends in a knoll. Go straight on, passing through a wide gap in a tall hedge, then descend gradually to a stream and climb a stile into another pasture. Go straight on for a few yards then turn right through a gate onto a surfaced farm track leading to a lane. Turn left and walk steeply downhill to Bredwardine, a small village set on the banks of the River Wye.

Go over the crossroads and turn right along a beech avenue to St Andrew's church which has some of the earliest surviving Norman work in the county, including some rare herringbone masonry. Its chief claim to fame, however, is its connection with Francis Kilvert, the Victorian clergyman whose published diaries record a vivid picture of rural life and society, both in his native Wiltshire and in the Marches. For several years he was the curate at Clyro, just over the river from Hay, and, after a short spell at St Harmon's in Radnorshire, he became vicar of Bredwardine in 1877. Sadly, he died only two years later, at the age of 39, and is buried here.

In the field next to the church are the earthworks of a medieval castle and a footpath allows a closer look, leading along the moat and past the manorial fishponds, some water still contained between their raised banks.

Return to the road and cross over to the Red Lion Hotel, a handsome brick building of the seventeenth century. Walk along a farm track immediately to the left of it and climb a stile by an old wooden barn. Continue along a track, going through a gate on the right into a pasture. Go straight across the middle, in line with a grey stone house on top of the hill ahead. When you reach two gates go through the left-hand one and go straight up a steep slope, passing two massive oak trees. Continue along the line of the ridge towards a farm, climbing two stiles to pass to the left of the farm buildings, but, once past the last barn, turning right through a gate opposite the farmhouse, then left onto a rough lane to reach a junction by Cherry Orchard Cottage. Turn right and then go through the first gate on the left which opens into Finestreet Dingle where a stream flows along the edge of a sheep pasture. Turn right to follow the stream until you reach a gate by another cottage.

Go through and turn left, going uphill by the hedge, then bearing slightly left to a place where you can climb the fence/hedge ahead (perhaps, by the time you read this, there will be a stile). Follow the right-hand hedge up the field then join a farm track which goes over two fields to reach a lane. Turn left and you very soon come to Arthur's Stone. This has nothing to do with King Arthur but is the remains of a late Neolithic chambered tomb, sometimes called a cromlech. Constructed of large stone slabs it is between 4,000 and 5,000 years old. Originally it would have been covered in earth to form a long mound and would have appeared much larger than it does now. It is impressive, but somehow less so than you might expect because English Heritage, which now has responsibility for the Stone, has destroyed any atmosphere or sense of history by surrounding it with a totally inappropriate fence.

A footpath behind the stone leads downhill, going across the middle of two fields then following the right-hand hedge through two more before going through a gate so that the hedge is on the left. Continue to the bottom of the hill and go straight on to Dorstone.

Arthur's Stone

14

The Black Hill

This is almost certainly the most spectacular and exciting walk in Herefordshire, and should be mandatory for all those who insist that the county is characterised by its 'gentle, archetypal Englishness'! Admittedly, part of the route is in Wales, but most of it, including what is by far the most dramatic stretch — the knife-edge ridge of the Black Hill — is very much in England. The views are simply stunning; the English Midland counties are spread out at your feet while Wales, to the west, is closed off by the seemingly impregnable wall of the Black Mountains. If ever a border looked the part it is this one.

Distance: 16 miles (can be shortened to 9½ miles — see note below).
Maps: Landranger 161. Pathfinders SO 23/33 (1039) and SO 24/34 (1016). Outdoor Leisure 13
Start/Parking: Hay-on-Wye, where there is a car park opposite Hay Castle, next to the TIC. GR 229422.
Public transport: Red and White Hereford/Brecon service 39 stops by the car park.
Conditions: Involves some moderately strenuous climbing to a height of 2,224 ft — but this is all completed in the first couple of miles and thereafter the going is easy. There is one steep, but not at all difficult, descent. There are muddy and boggy patches and shallow streams to ford. Wear proper walking boots and carry extra clothing. These mountains are dangerous and weather conditions can be atrocious at any time. Do not attempt this walk in poor visibility. Avoid summer Sundays and Bank Holidays.
Refreshments: Nothing available *en route* but plenty of choice in Hay.
NB: This is quite a long walk and motorists wishing to shorten the route can miss out Hay and Cusop by parking either below Hay Bluff at around GR 240377, or at the HWCC car park by the Black Hill at GR 288328. For public transport users Hay is the only viable starting point — and it really is worth the walk.

S ITUATED at the northern end of the easternmost ridge of the Black Mountains, Hay-on-Wye is a border town which used to be divided into English Hay and Welsh Hay. Today, Y Gelli Gandryll, to give it its Welsh name, is just inside Wales, although its suburbs are in England, and

The Black Hill

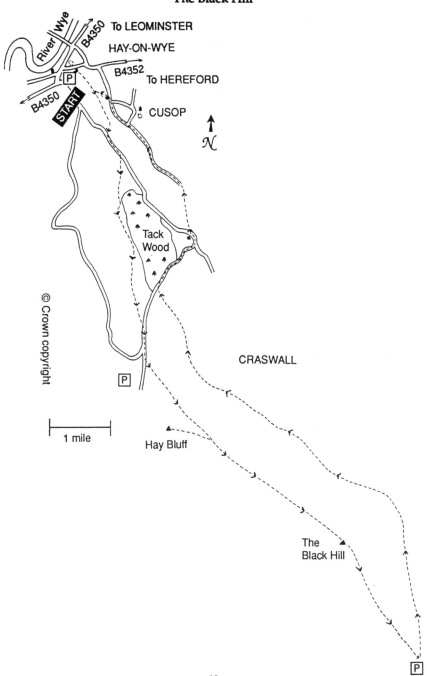

River Wye

B4350 To LEOMINSTER

HAY-ON-WYE

B4352 To HEREFORD

P

START

B4350

CUSOP

𝒩

© Crown copyright

Tack
Wood

1 mile

P

CRASWALL

Hay Bluff

The
Black Hill

P

its grey stone buildings and narrow winding streets are characteristic of small Welsh towns.

Hay's border position on the Wye has long made it a town of some importance and the Romans built a substantial camp here which covered 25 acres to the north of the river; today only some slight earthworks remain. To the south of the river, and close to the church, is a castle mound which was probably the site of a pre-Conquest fortification, but Hay is dominated by the remains of a later castle built in about 1150. Both town and castle were plundered and razed to the ground on several occasions; by King John, by Llewelyn the Great and by Owain Glyndwr, as well as by others less notable. The castle must have been frequently rebuilt, and in the seventeenth century a mansion was built within the existing walls, which accounts for its intriguing appearance today.

One of the more recent occupants of Hay Castle was bookseller Richard Booth, self-styled 'King of Hay' who turned the little town into the world's most important centre for second-hand books. Every other shop is a bookshop, including a converted cinema which claims to be the world's largest second-hand bookshop. People come from far and wide, not only to visit the bookshops, but also for Hay's annual Festival of Literature which has an excellent reputation. All this fame hasn't spoiled Hay; the retail and fast-food multiples which have brought a numbing sameness to Britain's high streets have yet to discover this small border town and it retains its own individuality and charm.

Turn right out of the car park and almost at once, just beyond a doctor's surgery, you will see a sign for Offa's Dyke Path. Go down a track into a field and go straight on by the left-hand hedge. Follow the well-worn, waymarked path across a further four fields then cross a stream by Cusop House and continue along the edges of two more fields until a waymark directs you across a field to a lane. Turn left and continue until you see the path indicated on the right. Follow the waymarks along the right-hand field-edge, cross a footbridge and turn left along the field-edge then over two more fields to reach a lane just to the left of a farm. Cross to the footpath a few yards to the left and go uphill, soon turning right then left to a stile onto a farm track. Turn left along the track, continuing even when it becomes the bed of a stream, to reach a gate onto open moorland.

The path is now less obvious but your destination is the peak of Hay Bluff which rises in front. Head towards it and when a road comes into view aim to join it close to where you can see a bend in it, near a row of trees. Follow the road uphill and soon after you pass a junction start looking for a boulder on the left which indicates Offa's Dyke Path.

Hay Bluff, at 2,224 ft, is not the highest of the Black Mountains, but it is

Hay Bluff – a winter scene

the most accessible and this can be a fairly crowded spot on sunny weekends. The Bluff is popular with hang gliders and paragliders so don't be surprised to see the air full of these enthusiasts.

The Path leads around the side of the Bluff but this area, popularly (and incorrectly) known as Hay Common, is criss-crossed with paths and nobody bothers much about rights of way. So choose your own route, but the easiest way to the summit is to aim for a path which rises gradually along the side of the ridge, reaching the top about a quarter of a mile south of the trig point. Keep going up until you meet a stony path. The trig point is visible from here and it's a short walk there and back if you want to stand on the actual summit. Return to this point and go left, or south. Offa's Dyke Path soon veers off to the right, to carry on along the main eastern ridge of the mountains, but we are heading for Crib y Garth, the Black Hill, a small tongue jutting out east from the main ridge. There is an obvious path which soon forks left from the path you are on. If you miss it, you will soon know because you will find yourself climbing to the next high point on the ridge. In this case, turn left downhill and you will very soon be back on track. The ridge of the Black Hill is visible ahead and it's impossible to go wrong as long as you remember that is what you are aiming for.

It is a little over two miles easy walking between the trig points on Hay Bluff and the Black Hill and the views are spectacular all the way. At a height of 2,112 ft the Black Hill is England's highest peak south of Yorkshire, and

Looking towards the Monnow Valley from the Black Hill

you can see from the Shropshire Wrekin to Gloucestershire's May Hill, with the Cotswolds, Malverns and all the rest between. On the Welsh side there are innumerable mountain ranges, including the Brecon Beacons, but the forbidding slopes of the Black Mountains make the deepest impression. As you continue south from the summit the ridge narrows and becomes rockier. It is known locally as the Cat's Back but though it's a funny-looking cat it is a splendid hill. It never narrows to the point of danger — this is no Striding Edge — but it is narrow enough for you to look down to the valleys on both sides as you walk along. To the east is the Monnow Valley, and to the west the Olchon Valley above Llanveynoe and Longtown. Outside of the Lake District, it's hard to imagine a more dramatic walk in England.

Eventually, you descend steeply towards a HWCC car park at the bottom of the hill. Don't go to the car park but turn back in the direction of Hay, only this time along the base of the ridge. There is an obvious bridleway which you follow for the next four miles or so to 'Hay Common'. At times it is a green lane, elsewhere it runs along field-edges, and occasionally it is surfaced. There are numerous gates, several streams to ford, and many turnings to the right. Don't be tempted by any of them; the way lies straight ahead and is quite clear. Just remember that you need to walk parallel with the mountain ridge to your left and you can't go wrong.

When you reach the open land below Hay Bluff the right of way goes to the left to join Offa's Dyke Path near the road. In practice, however, people wander freely on this unfenced land, and if you keep more to the right you can cut the distance down. In either case, aim for the road which runs over 'Hay Common'. If you bear right you should join it opposite a plantation. Just before the road is reached you pass an area known as Twyn y Beddau 'Place of the Graves'. Excavations have revealed vast quantities of human bones here, and tradition speaks of a great battle fought in the time of Edward I, after which the nearby Dulas Brook ran red with blood for days.

Turn right, walking by the side of the road, to a junction. Go left here, towards Hay, but very soon turn right by a yew tree opposite a farmhouse. A short, muddy track leads into a field and you turn left, going downhill with the hedge, and then a stream, a few yards to your left. Cross the Dulas Brook, which forms the national boundary at this point, to Cusop Dingle, turning left onto a rough lane. The wooded valley of Cusop Dingle is as attractive as it sounds but in 1921 it achieved a brief notoriety when a local resident, Herbert Armstrong, was hanged for poisoning his wife with arsenic. For years his likeness was exhibited in Madame Tussaud's Chamber of Horrors.

Walk along the lane, which closely follows the course of the fast-flowing Dulas Brook, with its mini-waterfalls and fern-draped banks. Cusop is a small, stone village with the earthworks of an ancient castle and a much-restored Norman church, next to which are some yew trees which were mentioned in the Domesday survey of 1086. If you want to look at the church and castle there is a footpath shortly after you pass Brynmelin, and you can return to the lane further along.

Just after a second road junction look out for Rosedale B&B on the left. Next to it is a footpath which leads down to cross the brook then passes cottages to a kissing gate into a small field. Cross to a second kissing gate and you will find yourself back on Offa's Dyke Path. Retrace your earlier steps across three fields to Hay-on-Wye, emerging by the car park.

15

Weobley

There is a small area of north-east Herefordshire where a handful of villages, set in some delightful countryside, contains perhaps the densest concentration of medieval timber-framed buildings in England. Weobley, the most southerly of these 'black and white' villages, is one of the most varied and interesting in the range of building styles it displays. This walk combines an exploration of Weobley with visits to the much smaller and lesser-known villages of Dilwyn and King's Pyon. Autumn is a particularly good time to do this one, when the summer visitors have deserted Weobley, and the surrounding tree-covered hills glow orange and red.

Distance: 9 miles
Maps: Landranger 149. Pathfinder SO 45/55 (994)
Start/Parking: In Weobley village
Public transport: Sargeant Bros. Hereford/Kington services 461 and 462.
Conditions: Very easy with no climbs but muddy in winter. One or two of the paths may be ploughed and planted over. A certain amount of lane walking is necessary because there are few footpaths anyway, and some of those have been obstructed. However, you are unlikely to meet much, if any, traffic.
Refreshments: The Crown Inn and the Village Stores at Dilwyn. A wide choice in Weobley.

WEOBLEY (pronounced Webbley) was founded by the Mercian prince Weobba in the sixth century as an outpost against the Welsh, and grew into an important and prosperous centre, its wealth largely based on glove-making and brewing. By the late thirteenth century it was in a position to send two MPs to Parliament — but this privilege was withdrawn when the inhabitants decided that they no longer wanted to pay the MPs' expenses. Weobley later regained its parliamentary representation but lost it again in 1832 when the Reform Act finally disenfranchised such 'rotten boroughs'.

Many consider Weobley to be the finest 'black and white' village in England and certainly, if it were not for the cars parked in the village centre, you could imagine yourself back in the seventeenth century or earlier. Some of the most interesting buildings are the Unicorn Inn, a rare example in the Midlands of the 'Wealden' house found in Kent and Sussex; the Red Lion

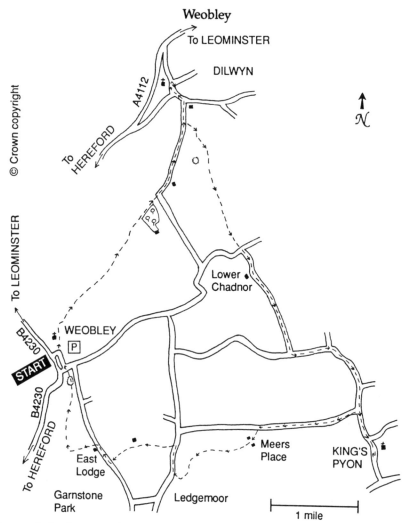

© Crown copyright

Weobley

To LEOMINSTER

DILWYN

To HEREFORD

A4112

To LEOMINSTER

B4230

START

B4230

To HEREFORD

WEOBLEY

P

Lower Chadnor

East Lodge

Garnstone Park

Ledgemoor

Meers Place

KING'S PYON

N

1 mile

Inn and the fourteenth century cruck-framed cottage adjoining it; the old Grammar School, now a private house; and the Village Stores with its timber-mullioned windows. The Mansion House was, in the sixteenth century, home to a James Tomkins who shared one room there with his two women and their thirty-three children, all of whom survived — a remarkable achievement, even in more prosperous circumstances, at that time.

Walk down the main street to the church, built in the thirteenth and fourteenth centuries in the decorated perpendicular style. It has the second highest spire in the county and is visible from miles around. It contains many

69

fine monuments, including one to Colonel John Birch, a leading Parliamentary figure in the Civil War who achieved the capture of Hereford. Despite this, he later served Charles II and became an MP for Weobley, living at Garnstone Park just to the south of the village.

Continue down the lane to a junction where you turn right to reach four gates. Go through the second on the left and walk along the field edge.

Although the surrounding country is mostly arable it is not flat and is pleasantly wooded. Cross three fields and enter a fourth, soon forking left just beyond a cattle shelter. Cross a stream into a pasture with some fine oak trees and follow the path to the far corner of a wood ahead. Walk left along the woodland edge and at the end of the trees continue to a gate on the left ahead and turn left along the lane. When you pass a pair of modern houses note a footpath on the right which is the route for later. Continue to a junction and turn left to Dilwyn, a most attractive little village with timber-framed houses clustered round a green. Its name means secret or shady place and, like Weobley, it sits in a hollow. At one time it belonged to the rebel leader Simon de Montfort but on his death Henry III granted it to his son Prince Edmund.

The church contains work from several periods but the earliest is the tower, built about 1200. A fine, solid-looking structure, it has tiny slit windows betraying its defensive role in days gone by — but an incongruous spire, added in the eighteenth century, detracts from its appearance.

Return to the path noted earlier and walk along the edge of an arable field, cross a footbridge and go straight ahead to a stile opposite. Walk left along the hedge then cross another footbridge and bear slightly right across the field to a stile. Over on the right a ring of trees encircles a moat and earthworks which signal the remains of an early, probably fortified, house. The next two fields may well have had the footpath ploughed and planted over. However, go straight ahead, eventually following power-lines across the second field as far as a large oak tree where the cables bear right and you go straight on to a gate. Walk down the lane opposite which climbs slightly to a junction offering a panoramic view of the hills on the Welsh border. Turn left towards King's Pyon. As you follow this lane the surrounding countryside becomes increasingly attractive, with the arable fields mostly left behind and a number of wooded hills rising in front.

As you enter King's Pyon notice Brook House with its timber-framed dovecote, sadly in a state of some disrepair. A little further on is the partly Norman church, set attractively on a small hill. Today King's Pyon is a very peaceful place, but it was not always so; the area was torn with strife during two civil wars — in the twelfth century when King Stephen fought the

Timber-framed houses in Weobley

Empress Matilda, and again in the seventeenth century when both Cavaliers and Roundheads made their presence felt with their looting and plundering.

Retrace your steps to a junction just north of the village and turn left for three quarters of a mile then left again down the drive of Meers Place, a brick farmhouse. You may be challenged here, but you have right of way. Turn right to go between the barns and follow the track to two gates. Go through the left hand one and walk along the field edge.

At the end of the field cross a track and climb a fence to the next field, continuing in the same direction. At the end of this one turn left to reach a stile between houses. It is very slippery when wet so take care. Go down a narrow passage and turn left along a lane then right at the next two junctions. Walk along the road as far as a wooden gate on the left under an oak tree whose branches spread across the road. Go through the gate and walk across a pasture towards the farm ahead. Continue across a second field until you draw level with the farm by a collection of gates and fences. Turn right here along the track to the farmyard and turn left along the drive. Walk to the road then turn right for a little way to reach a lodge on the left. Take the vehicle track just beyond it, following it into Garnstone Park where Colonel Birch used to have his home, now demolished. Walk along by the fence, passing through a gate, until you draw level with a gate on the left. Turn right here, following tyre tracks in the direction of Weobley church, now visible ahead. Climb a stile and bear right to reach the remains of Weobley Castle.

Founded soon after the Conquest by the de Lacys, the castle later came into the hands of the Talbots who held it for Matilda until King Stephen took it in 1138. It eventually came to the Devereux family, one of whose members was to achieve fame as Elizabeth I's favourite, the Earl of Essex. Today there are only some substantial earthworks surrounded by a dry moat. The footpath crosses the earthworks to emerge in the centre of Weobley.

16

Hergest Ridge

At nearly 1,400 ft high, Hergest Ridge is an exhilarating place where England meets Wales and you leave the cosy Herefordshire plain behind to stand on what, by contrast, seems the edge of wilderness. The ridge offers spectacular upland views in all directions, with the Black Mountains brooding darkly to the south. As Offa's Dyke Path traverses its length Hergest Ridge is well-walked in summer, but quiet at other times, and few walkers ever discover the paths which lead back into England via the ancient settlement of Huntington.

Distance: 10½ miles
Maps: Landranger 148. Pathfinder SO 25/35 (993)
Start/Parking: Kington car park, off the High Street. GR295565.
Public transport: Sargeant Brothers Hereford/Kington services 461 and 462. Primrose Motors Leominster/Kington services 495 and 497.
Conditions: The first mile or so is quite steep but otherwise this is not a strenuous walk. Conditions underfoot are generally good but it can be muddy in places. One short section may be overgrown with nettles in summer.
Refreshments: The Royal Oak Inn and PO Stores in Gladestry. The Black Swan at Huntington, open evenings only, from 7pm. An excellent choice in Kington.

KINGTON is a busy market town with an interesting history, although the experts disagree as to which king its name commemorates; some say Edward the Confessor, others prefer Offa or Harold Godwinson. There is a definite link with the latter, who, while still plain Earl Harold, subdued the unruly town after its menfolk had joined in a Welsh raid on Hereford.

Harold was merely the first in a long line of notables connected with Kington, and others include the great actor Stephen Kemble and his even more famous sister Sarah Siddons; the engineer James Watt who helped to bring the Brecon-Eardisley Tramway to Kington; William Wordsworth, who lived here for a time but, fortunately perhaps, never waxed so lyrical about Kington as he did about Tintern Abbey; and Lady Margaret Hawkins (née Vaughan), the founder of the present Grammar School in 1625 and the wife of that Sir John Hawkins who defeated the Spanish Armada. And not only

Hidden Herefordshire

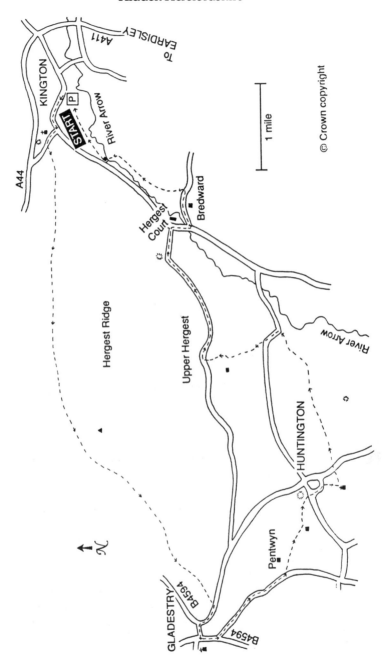

notables, but 'characters' too; locals still speak of Old Stafford the Drover whose habit it was to sleep in a broken tomb in the churchyard, and terrify early morning passers-by as he called out to them from his unconventional bed.

Nor was Earl Harold the only one to find the inhabitants troublesome, for in the 1830s Kington was one of the few places in Herefordshire to be involved in the Rebecca Riots, when protesters against the turnpike roads dressed as women and blackened their faces for their night attacks on the hated toll gates. They took their name from a verse in Genesis — "The descendants of Rebecca will possess the gates of them that hate them."

Walk uphill from the High Street to where the church sits in its isolated position above the town, revealing the site of the original settlement before the plan for a new borough in about 1260 caused Kington to move gradually downhill. Like others in Herefordshire, the massive bell-tower was once detached from the church, serving as a place of refuge for the population. Not far to the north of the church are the scanty remains of a castle, already abandoned by 1230. Beyond rises Bradnor Hill — a golf course on its summit at nearly 1,290 ft is claimed to be the highest in Europe.

Almost opposite the church, Offa's Dyke Path is indicated on the left, along a lane also signposted to Ridgebourne and Hergest Croft. Climb quite steeply uphill, ignoring any turnings, to eventually pass through a gate onto the short, springy turf of Hergest Ridge. Continue straight ahead, along an unmistakable path — wide, green and flanked by bracken — enjoying the

Hergest Ridge from the west

75

views which expand all the time as you climb, embracing all of Herefordshire as well as parts of other English counties, and a fair bit of Wales. The path is waymarked and you can't go wrong as long as you ignore all turnings. Eventually you pass to the right of the summit and the path begins to curve south and west as it descends into Wales. You might well see some of the hardy mountain ponies, known locally as Munts, in this area. Continue downhill to a lane, turning right along what is now Llwybr Clawdd Offa, and entering the tiny, grey-stone village of Gladestry.

Strange to think that Charles I and the tattered remnants of a defeated army clattered through this quiet place in retreat from Naseby in 1645! But Gladestry must have known danger and terror of its own long before the Civil War for the church, founded in 1060 under the patronage of Harold, has a sturdy square tower with tiny slit windows — unmistakably a defensive rather than a religious structure. Behind it stands a medieval tithe barn, also with slit windows, but with the unfortunate addition of a modern roof.

Offa's Dyke Path leaves Gladestry along a lane opposite a phone box and before long it turns off to the right while we continue along the lane as it climbs steeply to a bend by Pentwyn Farm. Take an overgrown path to the left of a ramshackle barn and follow it between hazel hedges until it joins a track by a farm. Turn left, following the track downhill and over a stream to reach the road by the overgrown 30 ft high mound of Huntington Castle. This motte and bailey fortress was built in 1228 by William de Braose, Lord of Brecknock and descendant of the 'Ogre of Abergavenny' who, in 1175, presided over the massacre of a group of Welsh chieftains whom he had invited to a banquet.

The castle passed from the de Braoses to the de Bohuns, to Henry Bolingbroke who became Henry IV, and finally to the Dukes of Buckingham. By Tudor times it was largely decayed and now only fragments of the stonework survive. Slight earthworks in the field to the south indicate the site of an abandoned village. The western edge of the castle stands on the present Welsh border and perhaps it is not surprising, given its position, that Huntington has two other castle sites within a mile of this one.

Go down the lane opposite to reach the village centre. It's a tiny place today but it was more important once and is mentioned in Domesday Book as having belonged to the ubiquitous Harold, before his close encounter with the arrow at Hastings. From 1403 until 1956 Huntington held a twice-yearly fair at which mountain ponies were traded. The tradition was that the pony which fetched the highest price would be ridden through the inn, a custom which was still carried out within living memory.

Turn left through a farmyard to the church which occupies a circular site indicative of great antiquity. Its dedication is to St Thomas à Becket and although it is sometimes said to have been built as an act of penance by Richard de Brito, one of the knights responsible for Becket's murder, there is no evidence of this.

Just to the left of the churchyard gate a second gate opens onto a path leading between fences then across two fields to the road. Cross to a footpath opposite and walk along the left-hand field-edge then across the middle of the next field, along the line of a grubbed-out hedge. After passing a pond keep to the left of the stream then climb a stile and continue by the hedge before going through a small gate and along the woodland edge. After a few yards climb a stile into the field on the left and continue in the same direction, shortly emerging on the road at a bend. Turn left to the next bend where you go straight on along a lovely tree-lined path which descends to a footbridge over Gladestry Brook and then climbs to a junction with a farm drive where you turn right to reach the lane at Upper Hergest. Turn right along the lane for nearly a mile to a junction where you will notice a mound opposite, the remains of yet another castle known as Castle Twts, a Welsh word pronounced 'Toots' (approximately!)

Turn right to the next junction. Opposite is Hergest Court, a timber-framed house which was, in the middle ages, the home of the Vaughans. The best known members of this family are Thomas, or Black, Vaughan, and his wife Ellen the Terrible. History has little to say against Thomas but legend has made him into a fearsome figure who terrorised the neighbourhood both before and after his death, when his ghost appeared frequently and in various forms. A group of twelve clerics finally exorcised his spirit which was contained in a silver snuff-box and placed at the bottom of Hergest Pool! Thomas's black bloodhound is also said to haunt Hergest and some consider it to have been the inspiration for Conan Doyle's *Hound of the Baskervilles*, especially as it is thought he did once stay at Hergest Court, and a Baskerville family certainly lived at nearby Eardisley. Conan Doyle, however, always denied it. Ellen the Terrible seems to have escaped the ghostly fate of her husband and their dog. Her main claim to fame is that she once cold-bloodedly killed a man, but as he was the murderer of her brother perhaps she can be forgiven.

Turn right, shortly crossing the River Arrow, and then turning immediately left onto a lane which runs alongside the river. Pass Bredward Farm then go through the second gate on the left, following tyre tracks straight across a field and continuing through a gap in the hedge before aiming for the far corner of the wood on the left. Go straight on along the edge of fields with the Arrow flowing below, eventually descending to cross both the river and a stream, keeping to the left as you pass through the grounds of a converted mill. At the road turn right at once onto a well-used footpath which leads through two pastures and across playing fields to Kington town centre.

17

The Arrow Valley

Like Weobley and Dilwyn, Pembridge and Eardisland in the Arrow Valley are part of a designated 'Black and White Trail' which highlights Herefordshire's most outstanding timber-framed villages, and attracts quite a number of summer visitors. Few of these stray far from their cars or coaches and the willow-fringed pastures of the Arrow Valley are little explored. The valley is renowned for its Hereford cattle, some of the earliest and most famous herds having originated here. The cattle share their pastures with sheep, occasional goats, and a variety of wildlife. The surrounding orchards make the valley especially attractive in the spring.

Distance: 8½ miles
Maps: Landranger 149. Pathfinders SO 25/35 (993), SO 26/36 (971) and SO 45/55 (994)
Start/Parking: In Pembridge. Park either in the old market place behind the New Inn, GR390581; or in a layby next to Trafford's Almshouses on the A44 at the eastern end of the village, GR394582.
Public transport: Very poor, best on Saturdays. Primrose Motors 495, 496 and 497 Leominster/Kington services. Lugg Valley Motors services 502 and 503 from Hereford or Leominster.
Conditions: Very easy with no hills. May be very muddy in places in winter.
Refreshments: Two pubs and tearoom/shop at Eardisland, three pubs and some shops at Pembridge, Post Office at Staunton.

P EMBRIDGE contains a wealth of timber-framing in a variety of styles and periods, and has perhaps more cruck-framed houses than anywhere in the country. It was once a town of some importance, its patronage by the powerful Mortimer family helping it to gain a charter in 1240, granting not only the right to a market but also to an annual fair which continued, in one form or another, until 1946, by which time the temporary closure of the A44 in order to accommodate the fair in the village centre was no longer acceptable.

Pembridge is still centred around its ancient market place and the open market hall, supported on oak pillars, survives, although it has lost its upper storey. The impressive New Inn was once an important staging post on the London to Aberystwyth road. It is thought that the 1461 treaty, negotiated

The Arrow Valley

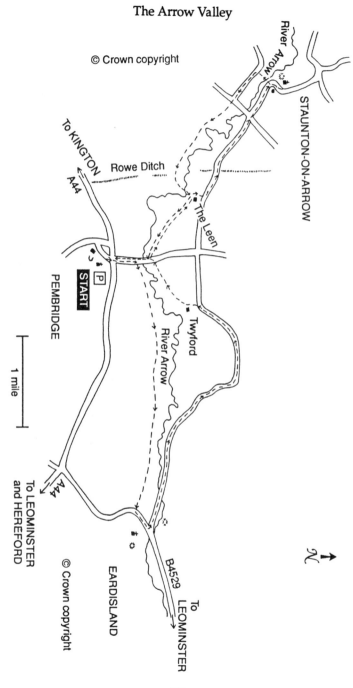

© Crown copyright

79

after the nearby battle of Mortimer's Cross, one of the bloodiest of the Wars of the Roses, was signed at the inn.

Behind the church, Court House Farm stands on the site of an ancient, probably pre-Conquest, castle. Part of the moat is still visible and the Court House has an impressive range of outbuildings, including a barn which retains the huge central arch through which loaded haywains would pass. There is rumoured to be an underground passage leading from the farmhouse's cellars to the church, a fourteenth century building with spacious proportions which contains some fine carvings of animals and mythical beasts. Its west door is peppered with bullet holes allegedly from 1645 when Pembridge was the scene of Civil War skirmishes. Its most remarkable aspect, however, is its detached bell-tower, of a design quite unique in Britain, but similar in structure to some Scandinavian churches and bell-towers. Pagoda-like in shape, it has three stages; an octagonal stone base, a weather-boarded section, and a short, shingled spire. The two lower stages are roofed with lovely old stone slates. Narrow loopholes in the stone wall reveal its former defensive function. Inside is a magnificent timber framework with eight massive oak posts providing the main support.

Once you have explored Pembridge it's time to head for Eardisland so walk down the road opposite the Red Lion and, just before the river, turn right, shortly going left over a stile to cross a meadow, aiming for a footbridge in the far hedge. Cross two arable fields, eventually following a stream to another stile into a pasture. Go straight across to meet the River Arrow, near a weir. It was not far from this spot that Henry Tudor and his army crossed the Arrow on their way to Bosworth Field in 1485, and Henry is reputed to have punned "He who would win a national strife must shoot the arrow first". Cross an arable field to a gap in the trees ahead and follow a stream to the far corner, looking for a stile hidden in the hedge on the right. Enter a pasture and turn left towards Eardisland, keeping close to the hedge, to reach a stile and footbridge. Go more or less straight across two fields, passing to the left of a short hedge, to reach the road. Turn left into the centre of the village.

Eardisland is one of the very few Herefordshire villages actually built around a river, perhaps because the Arrow floods less often and less severely than many. It is a chocolate box village with the river flowing between timber-framed houses, green lawns and colourful cottage gardens. Some well-fed ducks complete the picture. One of the very best buildings is Staick House which started out as a yeoman's hall-house in around 1300 and retains many original features. The seventeenth century Old Manor House is interesting too, and its garden contains a four-gabled, brick dovecote with 800 nesting alcoves. The Old Schoolhouse used to have the village whipping post attached to it and a pair of manacles still hangs from its timbers. Eardisland church dates from about 1200 and adjacent to it is the moated site of an early, probably wooden, motte and bailey castle. On the other side of the river is a much smaller mound at Monks' Court, which may be another early castle site.

Timber-framed house at Eardisland

To continue the walk, cross the stream and turn left to go between the stream and the river. Walk along this quiet, winding lane for two miles until you come to a sharp right bend where you turn left down the drive to Twyford Farm. Opposite the farm buildings go right through a gate and bear left across a field to another gate. Cross to the far corner of an arable field then go straight across a pasture to the road. Turn left then shortly right along a drive, continuing until a stile and signpost indicate that you bear right away from the drive, following the field boundary to the right of farm buildings and on in the same direction across the next field. Go through a rusty gate, cross a stream and climb a stile to a field, turning right along the hedge to the corner. Cross the dismantled railway line and follow the right-hand hedge, eventually passing a large farmhouse called The Leen. Reach a farm track where you will notice a stile opposite. A footpath leads diagonally right across two fields to emerge on the lane by the Rowe Ditch, but is currently obstructed at the far end so you may have to turn right to the lane, then go left along it. You soon reach the Rowe Ditch, a tree-covered earthwork which is obvious on both sides of the lane. It runs north to south across the Arrow Valley and is of uncertain origin, date and purpose. Most likely, it is a Saxon defensive boundary which pre-dated Offa's Dyke, here some four miles further west.

Continue along the lane to Staunton-on-Arrow, a small, mainly stone village, beautifully set in a particularly attractive part of the Arrow Valley. The Post Office sign – Swyddfa'r Post – serves as a reminder of how close Wales is, and many local people are of Welsh origin.

The church is sited on a small knoll overlooking the river, and contains a seventeenth century bible in a glass case. There are some interesting memorials; for instance, to Jabez Preece, church bell-ringer for sixty years, and to a one-time Deputy Lieutenant of the county who rejoiced in the name of James King-King.

Behind the church is a circular castle mound which rises to nearly 30 ft and is now rather overgrown. Church and castle overlook a ford where a Roman road once crossed the Arrow. Some years ago a Roman figure of the god Mercury was found here, but it may have been brought to the site by a former vicar who collected antiquities.

Retrace your steps along the lane to the last house in the village opposite which is a footbridge. Cross into a pasture and go straight on to a lane, turning left and continuing to a junction. Go through a gate opposite and follow a stream to its junction with the Arrow. Continue a little way in the same direction before turning right over a waymarked stile. Follow the field boundary and then the river. From April to October you should see many dragonflies along here, and it is good for birds at any time. The otter used to be common along the Arrow and, after a near-catastrophic decline, is once again showing signs of recovery, although you are most unlikely to see one.

The footpath veers away from the river, going past a small plantation to reach a waymarked stile. Follow the field edge until you come to a path junction. The Leen now comes into view again, as does another stretch of the Rowe Ditch over to the right. Another obstructed footpath causes us to retrace our earlier steps now, so go towards The Leen, then turn right to return over the old railway and across the fields to the road. Turn right into Pembridge.

18

Bircher Common

In the far north of Herefordshire the National Trust owns the Croft Estate and Bircher Common which together encompass about 1,400 acres, much of which is open to the public. Add to this the adjacent Forestry Commission holdings and the adjoining Leinthall and Yatton Commons, and you have a vast area of marvellous walking country with none of the usual problems of obstructed paths and difficult access. Bircher Common rises to 900 ft and the views over Herefordshire and its neighbours are quite superb. There is a network of paths to choose from; this is just one route which will suggest endless other possibilities for exploration.

Distance: 6 miles
Maps: Landranger 137. Pathfinder SO 46/56 (972)
Start/Parking: On the edge of Bircher Common at the top of Leys Lane (No Through Road) off the B4362 at Bircher. GR 470666.
Public transport: Midland Red West Hereford/Birmingham services 192 and 292 stop on the B4361 (½ mile). May be used in conjunction with the extremely limited Lugg Valley Motors service 491 Leominster/Bircher or Midland Red West services 493 and 494 Leominster/Presteigne.
Conditions: Good paths throughout. One slight climb. A little mud in winter. Avoid summer Sundays.
Refreshments: The Bull Inn, Stores and Bakery, PO Stores (mornings only, not Saturdays) all at Yarpole.
NB: Croft Castle is open April to October but not daily. Check times with NT. Park and grounds open all year.

THE 335 acres of Bircher Common contain plantation, woodland, scrub, bracken and grazing, with cottages along the southern edge. Grazing animals which may be seen include horses and pigs which forage for acorns in the autumn under the ancient system of commoners' rights known as 'pannage'. Bircher is rich in wildlife — look out especially for reptiles and birds of prey — and ablaze with pink and purple foxgloves in July.

From the cattle grid at the entrance to the common turn left past a house and walk up to a junction. Take the second right (heading towards Clee Hill which bulks large on the horizon) then in about twenty yards turn left by a young beech tree. Keep left, ignoring any turnings, along a wide grassy path with bracken and gorse bushes to either side. When you come to a major

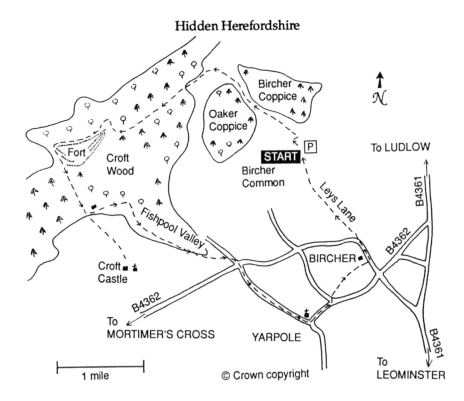

© Crown copyright

1 mile

To LUDLOW

To MORTIMER'S CROSS

YARPOLE

To LEOMINSTER

fork go to the right. The path leads between the trees, which include some fine oaks, to a crossroads where you go straight on, soon forking left to stay on the main track which now twists and turns to arrive at open grassland. Go straight across towards a conifer plantation, the top of which just shows above the crest of the hill. Turn left and walk along the plantation-edge to enter the Forestry Commission's Croft Wood. Go straight on then shortly fork right. Thereafter, ignore any side paths until the track bends left and there is a broad, green ride on the right. Go up here and through a gate onto Leinthall Common. Turn left and very soon left again over a stile onto an obvious path. At a junction go right and the path soon leads to the Iron Age fort of Croft Ambrey.

It has been suggested that the name Ambrey commemorates Aurelius Ambrosius, a Romano-British leader who may have been the Arthur of legend. Even if this is true there is no evidence that Arthur ever came here. It is a large, roughly triangular fort, well-positioned at 1,000 ft, and above the steep northern slope which overlooks Wigmore. Excavations carried out in the 1960s indicated that a fort was first built there c. 550BC but the present impressive ramparts date from c. 390BC. The traces of nearly 300 huts were

84

The detatched bell-tower of St Leonard's Church, Yarpole

found within the ramparts; together with signs of other buildings outside, these suggest a population of 800-900 at the time of the Roman invasion. As usual, the Romans burnt the settlement and the survivors were forced elsewhere, although a few later returned. Various artefacts found on the site can be seen in Hereford Museum.

The path follows the northern ramparts then descends to a stile. Turn left to re-enter Croft Wood and walk through it to exit in parkland. To visit Croft Castle go straight on, following the signs, but then return to this point.

The castle has been the home of the Croft family since the Conquest, apart from a break of 177 years. Parts of the walls, and the four corner towers, date from the fourteenth or fifteenth century, but the rest is eighteenth century. In 1746 mounting debts forced the family to sell the estate to Richard Knight, son of the wealthy Shropshire ironmaster (see Walk 20), and it was he who remodelled the house. In 1923 the Crofts bought back the estate and they live there still, although it is now owned by the NT.

Close to the castle is the fourteenth century church of St Michael which has an attractive seventeenth century bell turret and contains some fine monuments. A chestnut avenue to the west is supposed to have been grown from seeds found on an Armada ship wrecked off the Welsh coast.

Return to the entrance to Croft Wood and turn right (left if leaving the wood without visiting the castle) through a gate with red and blue waymarks. Immediately turn right, now following blue waymarks, and walk past a pink cottage, going downhill through attractive woodlands to reach the gorge of Fishpool Valley where you turn right along the lower path which follows the stream (red and green waymarks). Ignoring all turnings, go straight on, keeping to the right of the stream and a series of pools. These are rich in aquatic life and the valley has been designated a SSSI.

Eventually join the main drive to Croft Castle and turn left to a lane then right to a crossroads where you go straight on to Yarpole, a village which contains some beautiful houses. If you turn right at the junction just beyond the church you can see some of the best of them, Melrose Cottage for instance. A signposted footpath across a field behind offers further views. At the junction is a house with a medieval gate-house in its garden which, over the years, has served as a gaol, a Quaker meeting house and more recently, a bakehouse — the name by which it is known locally.

St Leonard's church has a detached tower rather similar to the one at Pembridge, though not so unusual. It is square with a truncated pyramidal roof and a short spire above a weather-boarded bell-stage. It still retains its original door and impressive interior timbers. The churchyard is partly managed for wildlife and is a glorious tangle of shrubs and wild flowers.

Turn left along the lane to Orleton and Ludlow, continuing to a junction by the lovely old Pound House. On the lane to the left is a gate into a field with a small farm building. The footpath leads along the left-hand hedge, along the edge of an arable field, then across three fields to emerge at Bircher, just to the right of Home Farm. Turn left, noticing a four-gabled dovecote, and Gate House Farm with its jettied upper storey, before turning right into Leys Lane to return to Bircher Common.

19

Wigmore

Close to the Shropshire border is an area of beautiful, hilly, well-wooded countryside which is redolent with history. Quiet and peaceful today, Wigmore was once the base of one of the most powerful and turbulent families of English history — the Mortimers, Earls of March, who, for 300 years, ruled not only much of the border country but also, on occasion, England itself.

Distance: 8½ miles
Maps: Landranger 137. Pathfinders SO 26/36 (971) and SO 46/56 (972)
Start/Parking: Limited parking is available in Wigmore village. GR 414690.
Public transport: Ludlow Travel Ludlow/Wigmore service 735 (Mondays). Primrose Motors Leominster/Leintwardine service 499 (Fridays). Teme Valley Motors Hereford/Leintwardine service 802 (when Hereford colleges are open).
Conditions: The paths are mostly good and there are no steep climbs. Some mud in winter.
Refreshments: The Post Office Stores, The Old Oak and The Compasses Hotel; all in Wigmore. The Royal George at Lingen.

WIGMORE today shows little sign of its past importance, despite the presence of some large, fine houses on its main street. Yet not only was it the seat of the Mortimers, it was also, for 900 years, the administrative centre for this part of the county, a position which was gradually eroded and lost during the middle years of the twentieth century. Only the ruins of its castle, out of sight of the village centre, now survive to recall former glories.

Opposite the Old Oak a 'No Through Road' leads to the large, Norman church of St James, which still retains some eleventh century herringbone masonry in its north wall. Its hilltop position and almost circular churchyard suggest a Celtic origin. From the north side of the churchyard there are excellent views of the castle and the flat expanse of Wigmore Basin, formed from the bed of a great lake which was caused by the melting of the glaciers in the final stages of the last Ice Age.

Continue along the lane which peters out into a footpath leading past the castle. Although privately owned, the castle may be visited but it is important to keep to the paths. Wigmore Castle is impressively sited on a

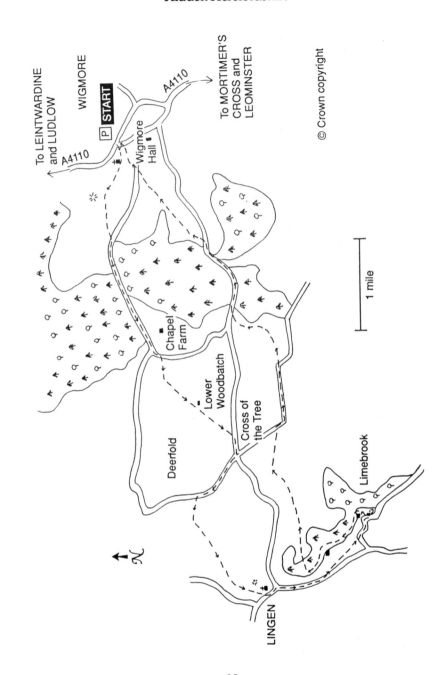

© Crown copyright

1 mile

To LEINTWARDINE and LUDLOW

WIGMORE

A4110

P START

A4110

Wigmore Hall

To MORTIMER'S CROSS and LEOMINSTER

Chapel Farm

Lower Woodbatch

Cross of the Tree

Deerfold

Limebrook

LINGEN

N

ridge and substantial portions of the keep, the bailey walls and the gate-house remain. Built by William FitzOsbern, Earl of Hereford, soon after the Conquest, it was granted to Ralph Mortimer and became the chief seat of his family. The castle saw action many times, the Mortimers being involved in nearly all the baronial wars and revolts of the medieval period, and in the early fourteenth century it was rebuilt, in its present form, by Roger Mortimer.

Wigmore Castle

For a time it was lost to the family as a result of Roger's treason. He was heavily involved in the deposition and murder of Edward II and, together with Edward's Queen, whose lover he was, he ruled England for a time in the name of the boy-king Edward III. Edward, however, proved twice the man his father had been and he had Mortimer arrested and executed for treason. Wigmore was granted to the Montacutes and the next Roger Mortimer was forced to marry the Montacute heiress in order to regain his patrimony.

By 1425 the male line of the Mortimers was finished but the Earldom of March passed through the female line to Edward, Duke of York, who, in 1461, sallied forth from Wigmore to win one of the decisive battles of the Wars of the Roses at nearby Mortimer's Cross, a victory which resulted in his becoming Edward IV.

By this time Wigmore Castle had already been overtaken in importance by Ludlow, and the colourful days of royal visits and great tournaments were over. The castle passed to the Harleys who later dismantled it during the Civil War to prevent it falling into Royalist hands.

Return to the main track which runs to the left of the castle grounds. It leads into a field and uphill, passing a group of trees, to reach a stile into another field. Continue to a lane and turn right, going steeply downhill through the forest. Look out for buzzards which sometimes perch in the trees by the road.

As you approach a junction you are entering an area known as Deerfold, formerly Deerfold Forest, which is not only very scenic but also of considerable historical interest. In the fifteenth century the forest provided sanctuary for the Lollards, a group of religious reformers who were heavily persecuted for their beliefs. One of their most prominent adherents, Sir John Oldcastle, is thought to have hidden at Chapel Farm (over on the left) for four years before he was discovered and executed. Deerfold is also of interest to the social historian for it has survived almost unchanged since the enclosures of the 1820s, being divided into numerous small fields, all with very regular outlines.

At the junction go straight on then turn right along a green lane which leads down to Lower Woodbatch — batch being a local word for a valley. After you pass a farm the lane is surfaced and goes uphill to a junction. Turn right and walk to a crossroads named Cross of the Tree, guarded by a large pollarded oak.

Turn right and descend the lane to a bend, soon after which a footpath is signposted on the left. There are superb views from here, to Woodbatch on the right, and Lingen on the left. Look out for deer which may be seen in this area. Follow the footpath to the right of a knoll then keep left to a stile. Cross a small area of scrub then walk down to the far corner of a pasture and cross a footbridge. Go diagonally right to another footbridge then diagonally left along a sheep track to the far corner of the field. Go through a gate and straight ahead for a few yards before climbing a stile on the left and heading across a field to Lingen church, passing a castle mound as you approach it. The church itself is not of great interest, having been rebuilt after a fire in 1891, but it contains some sixteenth century benches.

Leave the churchyard by the main gate, turning left then right into Lingen, a pleasant little village of stone and timber-framed houses. Notice the old yellow and black AA sign on the Royal George, which proclaims, with great precision, that the distance to London is 152¼ miles. Continue along the road, noticing Lingen Hall, a large white house on the left. As you draw level with it the road climbs slightly and at the top of the rise are two gates close together on the left. Go through the second one and turn right, following the hedge to a stile then bearing left to the lane (the path actually goes to the fence on the left, not the gate on the right).

Go straight on downhill to a junction by Limebrook Cottage. Turn right for a few yards to see the remains of Limebrook Priory, which was founded in 1189 for Augustinian canonesses by either Robert de Lingen or his Mortimer overlord. The nuns became very wealthy and owned a number of farms throughout Herefordshire and Worcestershire. Today very little survives of the priory; just some earthworks, fragments of masonry, and a rare plant, *asarabacca*, which is found in only a handful of places, each of them the site of a former religious house. It was a plant used in herbal healing techniques, and it seems fitting that the present occupant of Limebrook Cottage is a herbalist.

Return to the cottage, the interior of which incorporates beams from the ruined priory, and turn right along a 'No Through Road'. Pass an old, rather crumbling farmhouse then immediately turn left through a gate and walk a few yards uphill before going through an old, broken gate into a wood. The path leads along the woodland edge and is lined with foxgloves in the summer.

You soon pass to the right of Lingen Hall before reaching a crossroads. Go to the left, passing behind the hall then on along a forestry track. Go right at a junction and when the trees end climb a stile into a field and go straight ahead through a gate to a second field. Go straight on again then descend through bracken to climb a fence into a wood. Go forward to a T-junction. Turn left to a gate into a field then turn right and skirt the base of a knoll, crossing the field to leave by a gate at the far end. Turn right downhill and continue until the track crosses a stream and bends right. Go straight ahead along a green lane which leads to a tarmac lane. Turn right then left at the crossroads. There are superb views from here of ridge after ridge of forest-clad hills.

When the lane bends right go straight on along a track. This area is known as Mistletoe Oak; a reference to the fact that mistletoe, which usually grows mainly on apple trees, is quite often found on oaks here, a combination that was considered sacred by the Druids.

When you reach the lane turn right and continue to a footpath indicated on the left. Bear right past the corner of a wood, continuing to a gate near the top of the field. Turn right along the hedge and bear left to a gate, aiming for the far left corner. Climb a stile, go downhill along the valley bottom and cross a footbridge. Turn right, aiming for the far top corner of a large, park-like pasture. Wigmore Hall soon comes into view ahead, a fine timber-framed sixteenth century house. When you get to the top of the field there is an excellent view of the church and castle. Turn right then shortly left over a stile. Pass some earthworks and go straight on to reach a narrow, hedged path which then offers a choice of routes back to the centre of the village.

20

Downton Gorge

It's no easy task to choose just one or two walks in that remote and beautiful north west corner where Herefordshire meets Shropshire and Powys, but this one certainly has all the right ingredients — dramatic scenery, glorious views, charming villages; and the evidence of over 2,000 years of history, ranging from the Iron Age of Caractacus to the more recent iron age of the first industrialists. Not only history, but natural history too, with the red kite a possible, and very special, sighting. Having rescued this majestic raptor from the brink of extinction in Wales, the RSPB is now reintroducing it to England and Scotland. Locations were kept secret until, in 1990, an estate near Leominster hit the headlines when a gamekeeper was convicted of poisoning one of the young kites. It wasn't here, but it wasn't far away either, and this is certainly suitable kite country, so it's well worth scanning the skies now and again. You might not see a kite, but you're almost certain to see a buzzard or two in compensation.

Distance: 9 miles
Maps: Landranger 137. Pathfinder SO 47/57 (951)
Start/Parking: Leintwardine village GR405739
Public transport: Primrose Motors service 499 from Leominster (Fridays). Teme Valley Motors service 802 from/to Hereford (when Hereford colleges are open). Midland Red West Knighton/Ludlow services 737, 738, 739, 740 (infrequent). Hereford, Leominster, Ludlow and Knighton all have train services which makes travel to Leintwardine quite feasible from outside the immediate area despite the poor bus services.
Conditions: Mostly on good paths with a very little mud in winter. There have been path changes, mainly on the Downton estate, and although these are waymarked the arrows are, at the time of writing, incorrectly aligned! Follow the directions given here rather than relying on the waymarks.
Refreshments: Leintwardine has a fair choice — pubs, shops, a tea room, even a chip shop. The Sun Inn, where the landlady will serve you in what is basically the sitting room of her cottage, is often recommended for its unusual ambience.

LEINTWARDINE is a most attractive village with an old stone bridge over the Teme and a pleasant green nearby. Its houses are a delightful and unpretentious mix of styles and materials with stone predominating

92

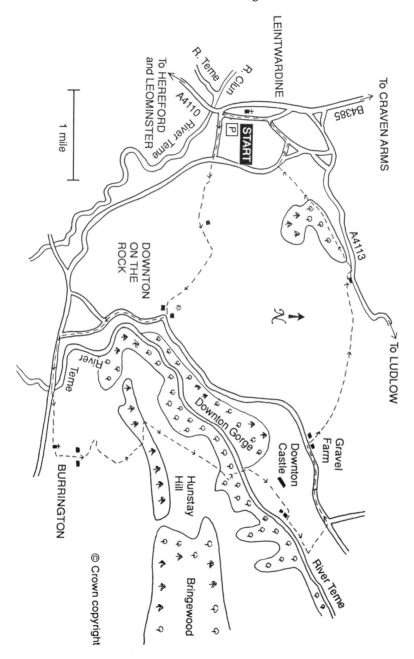

1 mile

To CRAVEN ARMS

B4385

LEINTWARDINE

R. Clun

R. Teme

To HEREFORD
and LEOMINSTER

A4110

River Teme

START

P

A4113

DOWNTON
ON THE
ROCK

N

To LUDLOW

River
Teme

Downton Gorge

Gravel
Farm

Downton
Castle

Hunstay
Hill

BURRINGTON

Bringewood

River Teme

© Crown copyright

93

— not just the usual sandstones but a variety of types in subtle shades of blue, grey, brown, cream and green, reflecting the complexity of the local geology. Beneath the village lies Bravonium, a Roman camp constructed during the frontier campaign of Sextus Julius Frontinus in about AD75. Traces of the ramparts and ditches are still evident over an area of about ten acres; notice, for instance, the bank on which High Street is built. The Lion Hotel stands on the site of the former Roman bath house and Watling Street, parallel to High Street, is part of the great Roman road of the same name.

After the Roman withdrawal the Saxons took over. A superstitious people, they believed it unlucky to occupy former Roman sites, but Leintwardine was in such an advantageous position, situated as it is at the confluence of the Teme and Clun, that they overcame their fears. The village suffered constant Welsh raids which continued after the Norman Conquest despite the presence of the powerful Mortimers at nearby Wigmore. The Tudor peace was followed by the Civil War when fighting raged nearby with the neighbouring castles of Brampton Bryan and Hopton both besieged.

Today, Leintwardine is a peaceful and interesting village to explore. It shows signs of having been planned, probably in the twelfth century, because its streets form a regular grid pattern. In the centre is the large church, inside which you can see the mechanism of what is one of the oldest clocks in Britain. Dating back at least to the sixteenth century it is made of wrought iron, wood, rope, brass and slate.

From the village green walk along Rosemary Lane, passing the Sun Inn and continuing to a T-junction. Climb a stile on the left and follow the hedge up a steepish hill to join a farm track and turn right along it, passing an old quarry. Already there are good views to the surrounding hills and the Iron Age forts on Croft Ambrey and Coxall Knoll, the latter being one of the many on which the warrior king Caractacus is claimed to have made his last stand against the Romans.

Climb a stile and continue along the field-edge then go through a gate to join a farm track. Continue past a ruined farm, soon climbing a barrier which extends across the track. At a junction go through double wooden gates and walk along an unexpected sycamore avenue. The large hill in front is High Vinnalls near Ludlow and there are good views all round. If you do this walk late in the year you will be constantly stumbling over pheasants from now on. They are so numerous and so unafraid that you wonder how pheasant shooting can possibly be regarded as sport.

When the sycamores come to an end continue down to the farm at Downton on the Rock. A little way to the north of it is a small motte and bailey castle site (on private land) and to the south half an acre of earthworks may indicate the site of an ancient camp (also private).

The bridge over the Teme at Leintwardine

Pass between the farm buildings to a lane. If you turn left here you can see the scanty remains of the twelfth century church which was abandoned when a new church was built nearby in 1861. To continue the walk, however, turn right and walk along the quiet lane for about three quarters of a mile. In places you can look down at the Teme below and if you look back you can see how the river has cut down through the soft limestone to form the sheer cliffs of Downton Gorge.

It's a beautiful view and it's strange to think that the gorge once rang with the sounds of industry in the days when there was a flourishing ironworks on the far bank. The noted Shropshire ironmaster Richard Knight moved here in 1685 and found it to be the perfect site; the Teme supplied water power, the nearby Clee Hills provided ironstone, and both limestone for smelting and timber for charcoal were abundant locally.

Ignoring a turning on the right, keep straight on to a T-junction and turn left. Cross a bridge then immediately go through a gate on the left and turn right to follow an obvious path which leads across fields to Burrington church. It is unremarkable in itself, having been rebuilt in the 1850s, but next to its east wall are eight unusual cast iron grave slabs, the earliest dated 1619. They commemorate members of the Knight family and feature interesting inscriptions and heraldic devices which have not eroded as stone would have done. It is worth going inside the church, even if only to have a look at the old tortoise stove which boasts "slow but sure combustion".

Cast iron grave slabs at Burrington

Leave the churchyard by the main gate and walk to the lane. Turn left, passing a farm to join a concrete bridleway which goes quite steeply uphill then makes a sharp right bend. Soon after this take a footpath on the left which crosses a field to a footbridge. Go straight ahead to a stile and cross the next field, passing to the right of a large oak tree and through a gateway onto a track. Turn left then straight across a pasture to where bracken grows densely along the edge of a plantation which clothes the slope ahead. Look for a faint path on the left which leads through the bracken to a stile into the trees.

Take the upper one of two forestry tracks on the left to reach the top of the plantation. Climb a stile to a field and go diagonally right to another stile close to the far right corner. Turn left down a track, over a stile on the left and diagonally right down a field to reach another stile and track. Turn right, fork left, and go through a gate then over a stile on the left into a field. Again go diagonally right to the far corner, passing a fenced area on the left. Go through a gate and turn left down a track which leads into Downton Wood where you will see a NCC sign informing you that this is Downton Gorge NNR, an outstanding example of a wooded river gorge.

The public footpath crosses the reserve but access to the rest is by permit only. Follow the path down to Castle Bridge over the Teme. There are beautiful views in both directions and it's a good place to stand awhile and look out for birds, especially wagtails and dippers. What you won't see is an otter, but they are present here. At one time otters were very common on the Teme, so common that the Leintwardine area was particularly popular with the otter-hunting fraternity — one of several reasons why the otter is no longer common. Since hunting was banned it has begun to stage a painfully slow recovery but its position remains precarious.

Cross the bridge and turn right along a track which passes in front of Downton Castle, a fortified mansion built in 1778. It was the home of Richard Payne Knight and was built to his own design. A grandson of the great ironmaster, Payne Knight was MP for Ludlow, a classical scholar, an antiquarian and a passionate advocate of the so-called 'picturesque' style of landscaping which developed from a revolt against the parkland vistas made fashionable by Capability Brown. Those in favour of the 'picturesque' believed in recreating 'rugged, wild nature'. Fortunately, Knight had little to do at Downton as Nature had already done a pretty good job herself. However, he did add some refinements of his own, such as an artificial cave and a 'Roman' bath house, as well as two fine bridges.

When you reach two houses on the right go down the slope to them and past the second house to a gate which gives access to the river bank. Walk as far as the next bridge then turn left along a lane to reach a crossroads. Turn left and after about half a mile take a footpath on the right. Go between farm buildings into a field, walk towards a large oak tree, and just beyond it you will find a fence. The footpath follows a farm track on the right-hand side of it, above the valley of the Stone Brook.

When you draw level with two pools down to the right the track passes through a gate, after which you bear left away from it to the top far corner of the field. Climb a stile and walk on, close to the left-hand hedge, through two fields. The path eventually curves to the right, to converted farm buildings. Go on to the lane, turn right to the road, then left along it for a few yards. Take a bridleway on the left which leads downhill through a wood to a gate where you enter a field and walk across, keeping close to the trees on the left. At the far end turn left then right through two gates and on in the same direction to reach a track. Continue to a lane, turn right and follow it as it curves round to meet Watling Street.

Bibliography

Andere, Mary. *Herefordshire, the Enchanted Land*. Express Logic, 1976

Catling, C and Merry, A. *Gloucestershire and Hereford and Worcester*. The New Shell Guides. Michael Joseph Ltd., 1990

Freeman, Barry. *Shire County Guide: Herefordshire*. Shire Publications Ltd., 1987

Gorvett, David and Lumsden, Les. *The Black and White Village Trail*. Scarthin Books, 1991

Johnson, Andrew and Punter, Stephen. *Walks and More*. Logaston Press, 1990

Minton, Jenny. *Access to the Herefordshire Countryside Today*. Minton and Minton, 1989

Pevsner, Nikolaus. *The Buildings of England: Herefordshire*. Penguin Books, 1963

Rackham, Oliver. *The History of the Countryside*. J M Dent and Sons Ltd., 1989

Salter, Mike. *The Castles of Herefordshire and Worcestershire*. Folly Publications, 1989

Salter, Mike. *The Old Parish Churches of Herefordshire*. Folly Publications, 1990

Scholes, Ron. *Understanding the Countryside*. Moorland Publishing, 1985

Tonkin, J W. *Herefordshire*. Batsford Ltd., 1977

Turner, J H. *Herefordshire Countryside Treasures*. Hereford and Worcester County Council, 1981

Various. *The Herefordshire Village Book*. Herefordshire Federation of Women's Institutes and Countryside Books, 1989

Recommended Reading

Chatwin, Bruce. *On the Black Hill*. Picador (Pan Books), 1982

Kilvert, the Revd. Francis. *Kilvert's Diary, 1870-79*. Ed. William Plomer. Penguin Books, 1977

Williams, Raymond. *People of the Black Mountains*. Paladin, 1989.

C000081208

PRAISE FOR DECISION INTELLIGENCE SELLING

"If you can use simple but powerful keys to influence people in your direction, whether you're in sales or simply in life, this is a must-read. Roy and Scott have written a new manual for sales training, a surprising page-turner for us all in leveraging our relationships to everyone's advantage. Bravo."

David Allen
International Best-Selling Author
Getting Things Done: The Art of Stress-Free Productivity—NL

"It was my very great privilege to work with Scott and Roy at a pivotal time in my career. Their practical approach and uncompromisingly straightforward style, grounded in a deep understanding of the human mind and immense real-world business experience, guided me to transform my division from an also-ran business unit to an exciting growth-engine. I continue to use their advice and techniques a decade later, in several companies, countries, and industries, generating success and growth every time. I recommend these powerful insights to anyone who isn't satisfied with mediocrity."

Colin Annette
Director, Technology Solutions, Qinetiq—UK

"Successful selling is a key factor in any business. Yet, surprisingly, neither BS nor MBA programs include sales as a key subject in their teaching programs. Even worse, most companies still stick to the old ways of selling. This book is great in describing in practical terms the way that any business should approach sales."

Gabriel Berczely
Chair GEBESA Holdings,
Hon. Counsel of Hungary in Chile—CL

"What is contained within this book profoundly changed the way I lead and manage my teams and has brought me more success than anything else I've learned in my career. This is not just a book about selling or a book about business but a set of tools to be used in all aspects of life. The ability to learn how to get yourself 'Above-the-Line' will be your greatest competitive advantage in a world where the pace of change is constantly accelerating."

David Brindle
Sr. VP Digital Solutions, EMEA, Hitachi Vantara—UK

"High-end B2B selling requires a new breed of salespeople, adept in the art of helping customers to make the best possible purchase decision. This book is a must-read for anyone who wants to join their ranks."

Roger Brooksbank
Assoc. Prof., School of Management & Marketing, Univ. of Waikato
Author of six books on business and marketing—NZ

"Wondering why your sales team is under-performing despite great hiring, technology platform investments, and training? Roy and Scott re-imagine the fundamentals of selling for today's world in a way all salespeople can understand, and most importantly, ACHIEVE. It's a very worthy read!"

Andy Cahill
Consultant and Senior Sales Executive—US

"Until I met Roy and Scott, I thought I knew a bit about sales. Having spent valuable time with them, I realized that I did indeed only understand a *bit*. This book is a wonderful summary of the vital insights they have. If you think you need to transform your sales function, read this book first!"

Mark Campbell
Consultant, Fmr. Europe Sr. VP, RGP Consulting—UK

"What a great book by Roy and Scott! Finally, something clear and easy to follow. Many so-called 'salespeople' are stuck with traditional sales strategies. I have no doubt that any salesforce will be reactivated and transformed by following *Decision Intelligence Selling*."

Sean Conley
President, Conley Global—US

"Well-written with a compelling sales and management approach that all corporate leaders should read. Reads like a nonfiction novel, hard to put down, and will surely leave the reader better able to fully grasp challenging issues—whether it be a sales proposal or a personal career change opportunity—before opining or pitching a solution. Absolutely worth the read!"

R. S. Cooper, JD
Fmr. COO, NASDAQ listed energy company—US

"This is a great and easy book to read, full of professional real-life examples as well as innovative concepts that salespeople should embrace to develop themselves. *Decision Intelligence Selling* is an eye-opener for all General Managers or sales experts who want their company and themselves to be successful."

Rodolphe Davezac
Deputy General Manager, CDK Global—FR

"Salespeople can be a key differentiator for companies in today's super-competitive business environment, but only if they do the right job for customers. Roy and Scott seek to transform sales into a profession that not only drives business growth and profitability but benefits customers and, ultimately, wider society. Let's face it, sales has long been due an upgrade. This book could prove an uncomfortable read for those simply looking for business as usual, but for business leaders interested in making the necessary changes, it is a practical guide."

Nick de Cent
Editor-in-chief, International Journal of Sales Transformation—UK

"Selling is not a magically improvised skill reserved for people 'natural' at it, but the result of a structured process and technique. Whitten and Roy tell you how to navigate this process and how to lead your team through the change as they deprogram the old automated habits and transform the way they sell."

Alfonso Emanuele De Leon
Fmr. VP APAC, Estée Lauder Co.
Author, Beyond Marketing—FR

"This deeply wise book stresses that you are born with the ability to change. It shows you how to reclaim that power, confront and liberate yourself from deeply ingrained habits, and connect to what is truly and elementally important to you. At the core of this book is a seemingly simple, but ultimately profound, notion of *transformation. Decision Intelligence Selling* guides you through a system so logical and authentic, you'll be moved to try it out and put it into practice as soon as you finish the last page. It just patently works."

Dr. Harry Dugmore
Senior Lecturer, Univ. of the Sunshine Coast—AU

"Do not read this book…unless…you truly want to transform the way the people in your sales organization think, feel, and embrace the concept of selling and the behaviors in which they engage. Many decent selling systems exist. *Decision Intelligence Selling* goes beyond these by addressing issues far deeper than adopting a set of processes that will guarantee an increase in your sales revenue. I have known Roy and Scott for years now and have seen them and their consultants succeed where many have failed by relentlessly living what is presented in this book. Follow their guidance and you will transform your salespeople and your sales results in ways that you might not even dare to dream about today."

Dr. Daniel J. Flint
Prof. of Marketing, Haslam College of Business, Univ. of TN—US

"As the CEO of both a technology and a wealth management company, I engaged Roy and Scott to work with both companies. The results were incredible. Their Decision Intelligence approach to selling has transformed the way we serve our clients and tremendously contributes to a positive and collaborative culture. The book is an indispensable addition to any leader's library!"

Greg Friedman
Founder/CEO/President, Private Ocean—US

"This clear and inspiring book highlights the most important principles that lead to incredible results, and it presents them in a simple, comprehensive, highly effective way. The unique R=A+C+E methodology opens a successful sales path to outstanding sales results. Enjoy your read!"

Mikael Garré
Global Client Director, Fujitsu—FR

"The prevailing paradigm of how buyers and sellers engage each other totally discourages young, enthusiastic, and energetic people from seeing business, and especially sales, as a noble profession. The brilliance of this book is that Roy and Scott approach selling as 'helping people think clearly'—about what they really want and what they really need—and then lay out the tools to accomplish that in a way that effectively grows the business in life-giving and satisfying ways. Brilliant and effective."

Ken Genzink
CEO, Genzink Steel—US

"DQ Selling has revolutionized our sales capability. We discovered a way of selling that not only delivered a significant rise in results, but it has created a sales culture and common language that has acted as an accelerator for growth. DQ Selling is straightforward, easy to follow, and as far away from intrusive or hard selling as you could ever get—it delivers a win-win experience and demonstrable results."

Richard Goold
Managing Partner, Moorhouse Consulting—UK

"In my experience, most sales books really boil down to a page of bullet points. *Decision Intelligence Selling*, though, isn't about tips and tricks; it's really—almost preposterously—about personal renewal. This book gets to the heart of why I do what I do and how to do more of what I really want to be doing. It makes me want to live up to the honor of having read it."

Peter Gross
Co-founder, Turaco Insurance—KE

"Roy and Scott are brilliant thinkers and wonderful coaches whom I've had the honor of collaborating with for over 35 years. *Decision Intelligence Selling* is a significant contribution to the field of sales in particular and human performance more broadly. Their awareness of how mindset affects performance and how people can learn to manage it for themselves—that alone is worth the read."

Dr. John E. Hoover
Psychologist, Business Consultant—US

"As a long-time executive coach, I worked for several years with Whitten & Roy Partnership as one of their senior consultants. I can verify from the inside that these two men practice what they teach. What they have created—for their clients and within their own company—is remarkable. Read this book!"

Sharon A. Hoover
M.A., Senior Executive Coach(ret)—US

"Shifting the focus of sales from 'sell what's on the truck' to 'help your customer make better decisions.' Roy and Scott live by their methods in this book, and it helped my team significantly improve the way we served our clients."

Mark Jopling
Fmr. VP, Global Banking, BT Global Services—UK

"This book is for sales leaders who want to help their people move away from a mechanical focus on 'pitching, countering objections, and closing' towards a more consultative, trusted, and value-adding model. It helps show how selling, done well, is a role that anyone can be proud of. Most importantly, it will help you help your salespeople become the best they can be and truly enjoy what they do."

Dr. Nick Lee
Prof. of Marketing, Warwick Business
School, Univ. of Warwick—UK

"*Decision Intelligence Selling* faithfully represents the transformation of our selling system at MicroEnsure. We had been frustrated for years trying to get a global sales team to sell as effectively as our two key deal makers, but to no avail. What amazed me was how Whitten & Roy Partnership helped us 'decode' the things we were doing well, throw out what wasn't working, and install the DQ selling method at the heart of our sales process. The complex deals that we have closed since that time are coming faster and with greater certainty than ever before."

Richard Leftley
Founder & CEO, MicroEnsure—UK

"If you're a company leader who wants to build a world-class sales operation, you've picked the right book. I know Scott's work firsthand. Thirty years ago, together, we built the selling system at Family Heritage Life Insurance that has stood the test of time and produced some $2 billion in assets. This masterwork needs to be in the hands of any leader who is serious about building a great company with sales flourishing at its heart. It challenges tired beliefs, instills new thinking, and lays out a sound and principled approach to selling with excellence and pride."

Howard L. Lewis
Founder/CEO/Chair(ret), Family Heritage Life Insurance—US

"I have spent my professional life assisting companies around the world to discover, hire, and develop high performers. I've worked with Roy and Scott for years, and their method is blessedly systematic and thoroughly sound. It works."

John Loven
President, MRA Enterprises—US

"Roy and Scott have written the best book I've ever read on selling—actually probably the best book I've read about business. The pages are steeped in practical experience and pragmatic humanity. If business is to survive in a functional world that we hope is just around the corner, it will be this shift to the deep understanding of, and care for, its customers, its staff, and its environment so clearly illustrated in this book that makes it possible. It may be a book about sales, but I can vouch from personal experience that the principles are equally powerful and rewarding in every business department."

Bruce McIntyre
Founder, Macpac, Co-founder, Seven Oaks School—NZ

"I have been fortunate enough to participate in sales training programs by Whitten & Roy Partnership. If you don't have that opportunity, read this book. The concepts are simple and transformative for both sales professionals and their customers."

Crystal Metcalfe
VP, global professional services org.—UK

"While this book is specifically focused on sales, the content is beneficial for *any* professional. The techniques in the book are valuable for moving from transactional to transformative in any relationship."

Lisa Mikkelsen
Head of Global Human Capital, Flourish Ventures—US

"This book takes me back to the excellent sales program Whitten & Roy Partnership led us through three years ago. Redesigning our sales process around the DQ approach improved our effectiveness, resulting in bigger deals and faster closing rates. Most importantly, we are now differentiated from the competition in the B2B solar market not simply by our products, but by how our sales force engages our clients."

Damian Miller
CEO, Orb Energy—IN

"WRP helped us discover our ineffective habits, took us completely off autopilot, and brought us together as a team. In their very pragmatic approach, they helped us manage ourselves and our sales force in a way that brought new energy, skills, and a confident mindset."

Willem Nolens
Founder, SolarNow—UG

"A valuable asset for everyone who wants to transform the way they sell. Read this book or someone who wants to take over your clients will. It is a guide to empower the next generation of salespeople."

Wilson Nzimande
MD, Founder Imithente Devel. Holdings, Realman Academy—ZA

"Having read many books on sales and sales management over the years, I can say this book is for CEOs and sales leaders who are *serious* about the importance of sustainable sales to the success of their organization. It's written by people who know the power, pain, and process of transformation and have seen it all. It's never been more relevant or needed than now."

Andrew Paten
Founder & CEO(ret), Metro Safety, Founder & CEO, UKNAR—UK

"Decision Intelligence is by far the most effective sales development program I have come across. Not only does the methodology lead to genuine win-win outcomes with clients, it provides the tools for salespeople to transform their results."

Steve Rathborne
Director, Partner Channel, BT Enterprise—UK

"When most people think about sales and selling, all they think about is profit. Roy and Scott taught me another way to think about selling: that it could foster wellbeing for both individuals and society as a whole. What they are proposing is a very important transformation of our assumptions and, for that reason, I recommend *Decision Intelligence Selling*. It may transform your thinking as well."

Stephan A. Schwartz
Editor of the Schwartzreport , Columnist, Explore Journal
Author, The 8 Laws of Change—US

"This book is exciting and revolutionary. It restructures the way you think about sales and managing the sales process. It proves that selling is more than pitching offerings to a client. As a result, the seller becomes a welcome agent of change rather than a necessary evil—a change that benefits both sales agents and customers."

Rob Shelton
Executive Fellow, Miller Center for Social Entrepreneurship
Author, Making Innovation Work—US

"This book is spot-on for the next generation of sales professionals. We need to sell in a way that puts the customer first by investing in and developing our talent and arming them with the critical sales methodologies to help them be successful. *Decision Intelligence Selling* enables this to happen."

Grant Van Ulbrich
Global Director, Sales Transformation, Royal Caribbean Cruises—UK